stashBOOKS®
an imprint of C&T Publishing

Customize with Accessories

Surprisingly Simple Projects with 3 Pattern Pieces

INSTANT SOFTIES

Isabelle Ewing

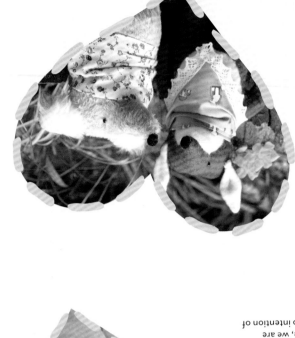

Text copyright © 2023 by Isabelle Ewing

Photography and artwork copyright © 2023 by C&T Publishing, Inc.

Publisher: Amy Barrett-Daffin

Creative Director: Gailen Runge

Senior Editor: Roxane Cerda

Editor: Madison Moore

Technical Editor: Debbie Rodgers

Cover/Book Designer: April Mostek

Production Coordinator: Tim Manibusan

Illustrator: Aliza Shalit

Photography Coordinator: Lauren Herberg

Production Assistant: Rachel Ackley

Photography by Stacy Grant

Pattern on pages 8, 28, and 76 provided by MOJX Studio/Shutterstock.com

Published by Stash Books, an imprint of C&T Publishing, Inc., P.O. Box 1456, Lafayette, CA 94549

Library of Congress Cataloging-in-Publication Data

Names: Ewing, Isabelle, author.

Title: Instant softies : surprisingly simple projects with 3 pattern pieces / Isabelle Ewing.

Description: Lafayette, CA : Stash Books, [2023] | Summary: "With the simple three piece pattern system, even complete beginners can sew adorable animal softies in just a few hours. Inside features 7 cute characters to make and dress such as a bear, a fox, an elephant, a mouse and more"-- Provided by publisher.

Identifiers: LCCN 2022047207 | ISBN 9781644033692 (trade paperback) | ISBN 9781644033708 (ebook)

Subjects: LCSH: Soft toy making--Patterns. | Stuffed animals (Toys)--Patterns. | Animals in art.

Classification: LCC TT174.3 .E95 2023 | DDC 745.592/4--dc23/eng/20221013

LC record available at https://lccn.loc.gov/2022047207

Printed in China

10 9 8 7 6 5 4 3 2 1

Dedication

This book is dedicated to all the creative people out there who bring such beauty into our lives.

Acknowledgment

I would like to thank my husband, Alan, for being the IT guy on this book. As a self-confessed technophobe, I can honestly say he had his work cut out for him from the word go (and then some). Thanks, Big Guy. x x x

A special thank you to the wonderful people at C&T publishing. They were always there to sort out any queries and keep me on the right track. Their kindness and help made writing this book a very positive experience. A heartfelt thank you to you all.

Contents

Introduction ♥ 6

Section One: Basic Techniques ♥ 8

Section Two: Animals ♥ 28

TEDDY BEAR SOFTIE
McBear

30

ELEPHANT SOFTIE
Nellyphant

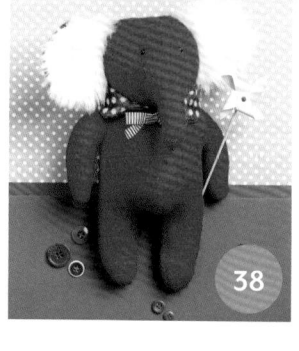
38

MOUSE SOFTIE
Little Mouse

44

FOX SOFTIE
Fab Foxy

50

DOG SOFTIE
Woofy

56

HORSE SOFTIE
Neddykins

62

RABBIT SOFTIE
Robin

70

Section Three: Outfits and Accessories ♥ 76

SHOULDER BAG

78

COLLAR

80

RUFFLE

82

SCARF

84

SHAWL

86

TOP HAT

88

BOW

92

Patterns ♥ 94

About the Author ♥ 111

INTRODUCTION

Welcome to my book! We're going to cover how to make seven enchanting softies, each using only three pattern pieces. The book is split into three main sections. The first is simple: basic techniques for reading and preparing the templates. The second section is where things get exciting: you get to choose and create your animal character! And finally, in the third section, you decide how to accessorize your softie (if you want to!). Each animal is simple, customizable, and as sweet as can be.

I wrote this book because I have a love for crafting, and I want to share it with others. This book is suitable for those who have never crafted before, as each step is explained clearly and in great detail. I know that by the end of the book, you will feel confident about stitches, pattern marks, and all the relevant techniques necessary to make every project an outstanding success.

Many people think you need to be able to paint the Sistine Chapel to be an artist, but that couldn't be further from the truth. Just like learning to drive or swimming in the deep end, you start by learning a simple skill and build on it. This book is one building block for constructing a creative future.

Advanced crafters will also love how quick these little characters are to make. So, surprise yourself and others by making these animals. The best part is that they are **fun, fun, fun**!

So, let's get going.

1

Basic Techniques

This is the start of your simple softie journey! Within this section, I cover the project preparation phase. It's best to have everything at hand before starting to cut and sew.

9

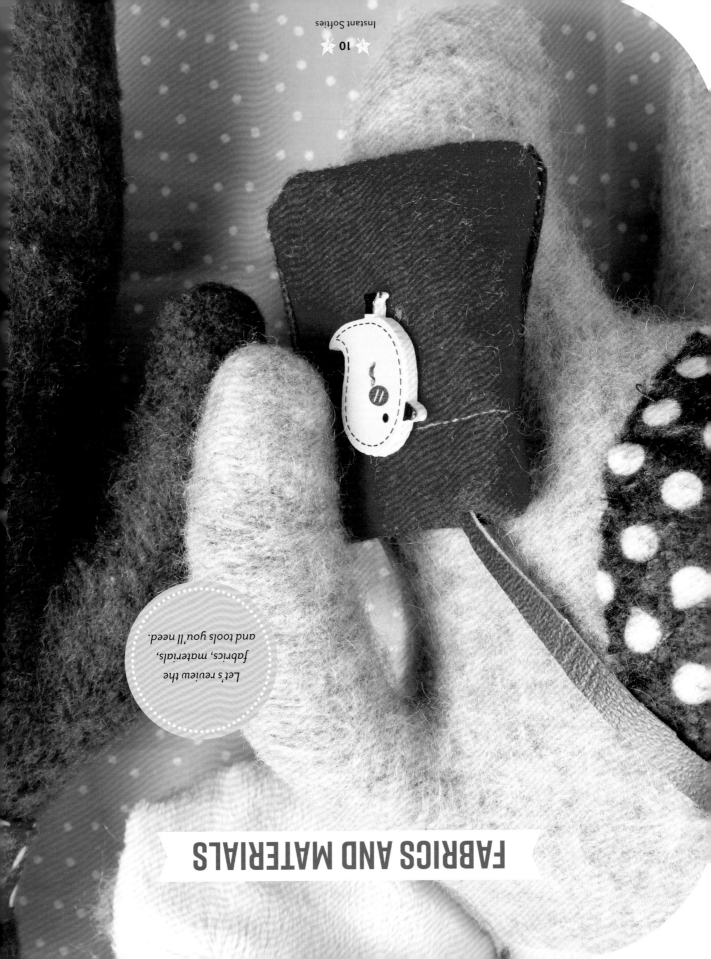

Let's review the fabrics, materials, and tools you'll need.

FABRICS AND MATERIALS

Fabrics

There are a variety of suitable fabrics for making up the little animals in this book. I have listed a few of my favorite options below.

Kunin Plush Felt

Kunin *plush* felt (available at kuninfelt.com) is thicker than regular felt, and it has a raised pile, meaning it is not completely flat like regular Kunin felt. This plush felt is my favorite fabric to use for these projects because it is easy to cut and sew. It also comes in a wide variety of colors, so it will work for any of the animals. It's made from 100% recycled postconsumer plastic bottles. This fabric can sometimes stretch more than you'd like it to, so be careful when stuffing your plush felt softies. I highly recommend that you use Kunin plush felt.

Cuddle Fleece

Cuddle fleece fabric is super soft and durable, and it comes in a myriad of colors. It's easy to both cut and sew, and it does not fray. This is a great option if you're looking to make a softie that is great for cuddling. Notes to remember when using cuddle fleece:

- The right and wrong sides of the fabric can be very similar, so be careful and consistent when choosing the right side. In general, you *can* use either side of the fabric, but you want to make sure all the pieces of your softie match.

- Cuddle fleece fabric has a longer pile than plush felt, and it can be hard to spot the direction of the pile. You'll notice that if you brush it one way it looks lighter, and if you brush it the other way it looks darker. We'll learn more about pile and why it's important later; see Direction of the Fabric Pile (page 21).

Felt

I prefer to use standard felt for many of the accessories. A wool/viscose blend is best. Acrylic felt should be avoided; it is usually thin and does not hold its shape.

More About Choosing a Fabric

1. Any fabric that has a relatively short pile can be used. Fabric with a longer pile will make cutting and sewing much more difficult and is not suitable for these projects. You want the fabric to feel fuzzy, not furry.

2. You can find suitable fabrics in craft stores or online. If you can't head to a store to actually see and feel the fabric, most retailers offer a swatch service, which is very helpful for trying new fabrics. Buy small amounts of fabrics until you decide which you like working with best.

3. Your fabric should be soft and pliable. You'll need it to fold easily while you're making your softie, and you want it to be nice to hold and squeeze after it's finished.

Needles

You will need three needles:

- ♥ A standard sharp hand-sewing needle for sewing the fabric together

- ♥ A large-eyed sharp hand-sewing needle for embroidery

- ♥ A long (approximately 3"), sharp hand-sewing needle, sometimes called a doll needle, for sewing the eye buttons

You will be able to find all three types of needles in a craft store, online, or maybe even around the house.

Thread

You will also need three types of thread:

- ♥ Standard all-purpose thread that matches the color of your chosen fabric, for sewing the softie together

- ♥ Black embroidery thread, for embroidering the face

- ♥ Black extra-strong thread, for sewing on the eye buttons

You will be able to find all three types of thread in a craft store or online. If you want to reduce the number of colors you need to purchase, I suggest sticking with browns, grays, and whites.

Stuffing

You can use any kind of toy or pillow stuffing to fill your softies. The most common kind is polyester fiberfill, which is what I use.

Long Sewing Pins

Ordinary sewing pins will work fine, but long sewing pins will be easier to use for these projects. I also recommend buying pins with colored heads, which will make it easier to keep track of them in your project.

Sew-On Eyes

Each softie will need a pair of plastic sew-on eyes. Eyes around ¼˝ (6mm) will fit well. Try finding them on Etsy or at a local craft shop. If you prefer, you can also forgo these materials and use embroidery thread to stitch two black dots for eyes. Embroidered eyes are the safer choice if you choose to make a softie for a young child. Never share a softie with detachable parts or accessories with an infant.

Scissors

You will need a sharp pair of scissors that you use exclusively for cutting thread and fabric. You never want to use your sewing scissors for cutting paper or other materials, or they'll get dull fast! Fleece is especially difficult to cut without sharp scissors.

Fabric Pen

To mark your fabric, you will need a water-erasable fabric pen. Marks from this type of fabric pen will disappear with water.

Black Pom-Poms

Small black pom-poms make the perfect noses for these adorable softies. Look for options that are about ⅜˝ (10mm) in size, online or at your local craft store. Larger black or brown pom-poms, 1¼˝ (30mm), can also be used for the horse's mane.

Pink or Red Colored Pencil

I love adding a bit of blush to the cheeks of some softies. Any kind of watercolor pencil in pink or red will work.

BASIC SEWING

The projects in this book are all hand sewn using five basic stitches. Let's review each stitch, along with some basics for preparing your needle and thread. The pieces that make up the softie and accessories are small and can be fiddly to sew on a sewing machine, but if you prefer to go that route, it is possible.

Threading the Needle

First, always try to select a standard all-purpose thread that matches your fabric. You don't want the thread to stand out on the finished softie.

For all the projects in this book, double thread the needle for increased security. Let's practice:
Cut a piece of thread to 24˝ (61cm). Feed one end of the thread through the eye of a standard needle and pull so the two ends meet each other. Knot the two tails together. Now your needle is double threaded!

Double Stitching

I recommend starting and finishing every line of stitches with a double stitch. A double stitch will give your work more security, strength, and durability.

To make a double stitch, first make a small single backstitch. Bring your threaded needle from back to front through your fabric (A), and then again from front to back about ¼˝ (6mm) to the right to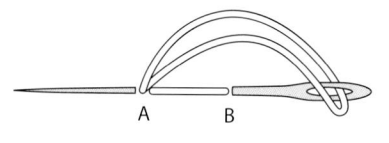
make a stitch (B). Then, make a second stitch directly on top of the first stitch. Bring your needle from back to front through the same hole you started with (A), and then back down from front to back in the second hole you created (B). Now you have two stitches directly on top of each other, and you're ready to use any of the basic stitches. Repeat this process at the end of your line of stitches.

Basic Stitches

To get a feel for each of these stitches, thread a needle, grab a piece of scrap fabric, and follow along.

Running stitch

Slip stitch

Satin stitch

Backstitch

Whipstitch

The Running Stitch

The running stitch is probably the simplest hand stitch. To make a running stitch, bring your threaded needle through your fabric from back to front (A). Bring your needle through the fabric from front to back about ¼˝ (6mm) to the left of the first point (B), and then back to the front about ¼˝ (6mm) to the left again (C).

Repeat this process to create a line of stitches. You can adjust the distance between points to suit your project. The closer the points are to each other, the more secure your line of stitches will be.

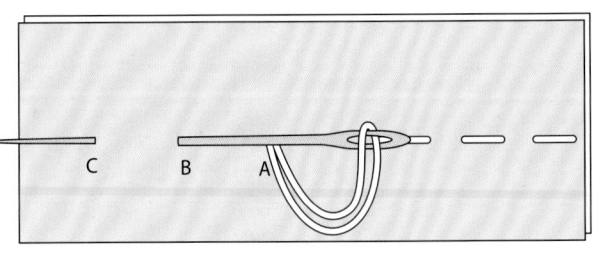

Needle stitches from back to front at point A, from front to back at point B, and again from back to front at point C. Repeat to continue making running stitches.

The Backstitch

The backstitch is the strongest hand stitch, which makes it great for creating a secure seam. Unless specifically noted otherwise, this stitch will be used for all the seams in this book.

To make a backstitch, bring your threaded needle through your fabric from back to front (A). Choose a point about ¼˝ (6mm) to the right of the first point (B) and bring your needle back through the fabric from front to back to create your first stitch. Choose a third point about ¼˝ (6mm) to the left of A and bring the needle through the fabric from back to front (C).

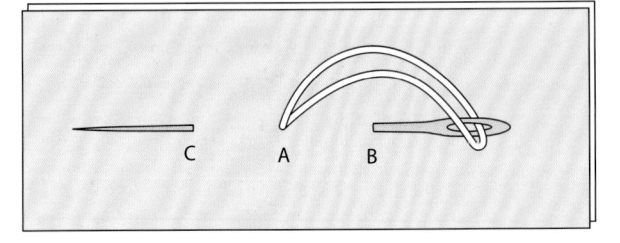

Now, bring your needle from front to back through the first hole (A), creating two connected stitches. Bring your needle from back to front to the left of the last hole (C). Repeat this process to create a line of backstitches.

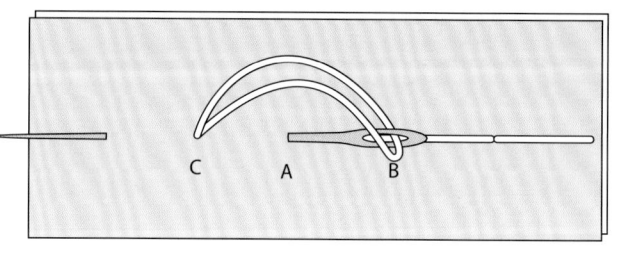

Needle stitches from back to front at point A, from front to back at point B, from back to front at point C, and then from front to back at point A and continue to left of point C.

The Slip Stitch

The slip stitch is used for closing holes, for stitching hems, and for attaching ears. This stitch is nearly invisible and is very strong when the stitches are kept small and close together.

You use a slip stitch when you need to stitch two pieces of fabric together. Fold the edges of each piece of fabric under ¼″ (6mm) and adjust so the folded edges line up. Insert your threaded needle from back to front on the top piece of fabric (A). Then, directly across on the bottom piece of fabric, push the needle through the front side of the fabric (B) and reemerge about ⅛″ (3mm) to the left (C). Continue directly across on the top piece of fabric and push the needle through the front side of the fabric and reemerge about ⅛″ (3mm) to the left. Pull the thread through, joining the 2 pieces of fabric together. Continue stitching as needed until the 2 pieces are firmly attached (or, in a project, until the hole is closed).

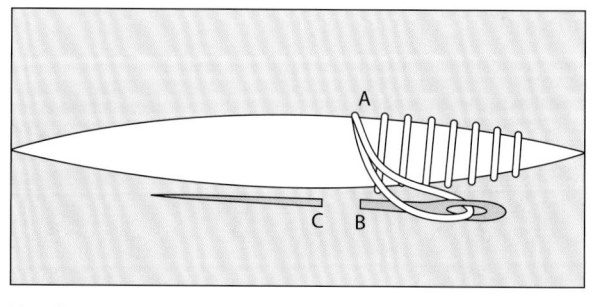

Needle stitches from front to back to front on top piece of fabric; then, on bottom piece of fabric, needle stitches from front to back to front again.

The Whipstitch

The whipstitch is also used primarily to join multiple layers of fabric together at an edge.

To make a whipstitch, prepare two pieces of fabric and place the edge of the top fabric about 1″ (2.5cm) from the edge of the bottom fabric. Insert the needle from back to front on the top piece of fabric (A). Then, insert the needle from front to back through the bottom fabric at a slight angle to create the first stitch (B). Bring the needle from back to front through both pieces of fabric, still at a slight angle, about ¼″ (6mm) to the left of the first stitch (C). Repeat the stitching over the edge of the top fabric.

Needle stitches from back to front of top fabric at point (A), then, at slight angle, from front to back of bottom fabric at point (B), and then up through both fabrics at point (C).

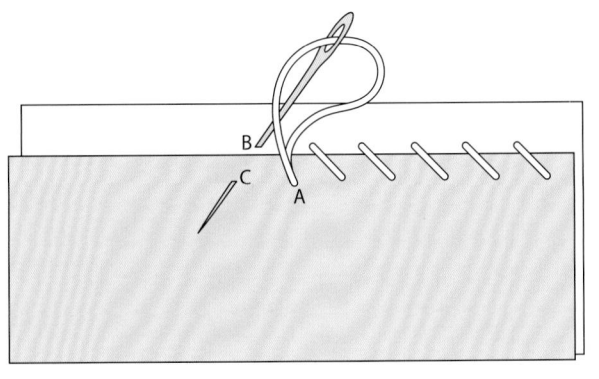

The Satin Stitch

The satin stitch is used to fill in a block of space. In these projects, you'll have the option of using it to embroider the noses of McBear, Little Mouse, Fab Foxy, Woofy, and Robin, as well as the eyes of any of the softies if you choose not to sew on button eyes.

To make a satin stitch, first plan an area you want to fill. I suggest practicing with a small rectangle. Mark the shape or its four corners on the fabric with a pen or pencil. Bring the threaded needle from back to front at one corner of the rectangle (A); then bring the needle to an adjacent corner (B) and stitch from front to back to create the first satin stitch. Note that the corner you choose will determine the direction of your satin stitches. Push the needle through the fabric from back to front right next to the first hole (C), and then bring it down from front to back right next to the second hole (D) to complete two adjacent satin stitches. Repeat until the space is filled.

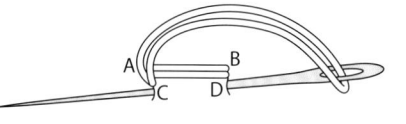

Needle stitches from back to front at point (A) and from front to back at point (B). Repeat at points (C) and (D) to create second satin stitch. Repeat to fill shape.

More Sewing Tips and Reminders

These tips will help keep your project on the right track and prevent problems.

- When sewing two pieces of fabric or a seam together, always take the time to securely pin the pieces together. This will keep the fabric from moving when you are sewing.

- Make sure you always leave space between your stitches and the edge of the fabric. This is called a seam allowance. All seam allowances for the softies should be ¼″ (6mm).

- Don't forget to start and end each line of stitches with a double stitch.

- Keep your stitches evenly spaced. Remember that the closer together your stitches are, the stronger they are.

- After each stitch, make sure the thread is pulled all the way through the fabric and the stitch is lying flat.

- Check your work as you go! Looking out for errors and referring back to this checklist every so often will keep you from finishing a project without realizing you accidentally left a gap or sewed a seam too close to the edge.

UNDERSTANDING PATTERNS

Sewing patterns are the templates that you'll follow to make each softie. The patterns in this book are very simple, but there are still a few important things to know about them before you start using them.

Pattern Marks

Pattern marks are symbols that appear on the pattern to indicate something about how you should make your softie. Before cutting out the pieces (more on that soon), you'll want to transfer the marks from the pattern to the fabric. Use a fabric pen to copy over each pattern mark carefully before you start cutting.

Let's review each of the marks that will appear in this book.

Direction of the Fabric Pile

The raised fiber surface of a fabric like plush felt or cuddle fleece is called pile. Getting the pile direction right is crucial for the look of the finished project! All the pile in a project needs to lie in the same direction for the softie to have a uniform and polished appearance. To determine a fabric's pile direction, think of a dog's fur: when you brush it one way, it lies flat and smooth, but if you brush it the other way, it will resist and stick up. The arrow refers to the direction of the fabric's pile that feels smooth and flat when you run your hand over it. Position the fabric so that the smooth direction goes from top to bottom. Place the pattern pieces on top of the fabric, with the "direction of pile" arrow pointing down. Use this arrow to ensure that all the pile on the softie is lying in that same top-to-bottom direction.

Cut on Fold of Fabric

The back pieces for all the softies should be cut out from a piece of fabric that is folded in half (see Cutting the Fabric Pieces, page 23). The double-ended "cut on fold of fabric" arrow indicates how to arrange the pattern piece in relation to the fold. Place the straight edge of the pattern piece on top so that the arrows line up with the fold. Then, when you cut the piece, you will get two symmetrical halves connected by the fold.

Matching Pattern Pieces

When you begin to assemble a softie, you'll need to match certain parts of the fabric pieces together. A letter with a dot indicates the place where you should match two pieces together. So, for example, look for dot **A** on one fabric piece to match with dot **A** on a different fabric piece.

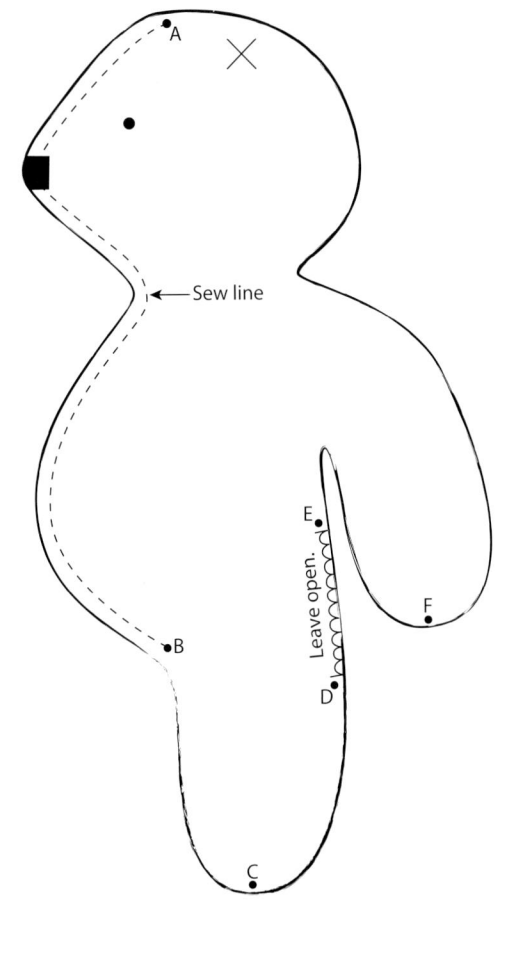

Sew Line

The dashed sew line indicates where you should sew on the fabric. Unless otherwise indicated, you will sew with a backstitch on this line.

Leave Open

The scalloped "leave open" symbol indicates that you should leave a gap in a seam. So, don't sew where this symbol appears.

Ear Point

The large **X** indicates where the ear should be placed on the softie's head.

Pattern Pieces

Each softie needs three pattern pieces: a back, a front, and an ear.

Cutting the Template Pieces

All the pattern pieces for the softies and accessories are found in Patterns (page 94). Photocopy, trace, or print the patterns you need for each softie, and cut each one out to make your templates. A few of the patterns are in two parts and will need to be taped or traced together. You may use regular paper for the templates or make more durable ones. I like to trace my patterns onto a piece of sturdy card stock or cardboard. It's easier to trace around a thicker template, and it won't be as easily damaged as paper. I find it well worth the extra effort of doing this, especially since I make these softies over and over.

Review the patterns to spot and identify the pattern marks. Use them with the following directions to cut out the fabric pieces for your softies.

Cutting the Fabric Pieces

It's important to follow the pattern layout and place the template pieces on the fabric correctly. This helps make sure both that you're making the best use of your fabric and that you're cutting the right number of pieces.

1️⃣ Cut out a rectangle of fabric that is 14″ × 28″ (35.6cm × 71.1cm). Lay it out right side up. If you prefer, you can also just cut the pieces from a ½ yard piece of fabric.

2️⃣ Fold the fabric in half so that it now measures 14″ × 14″ (35.6 × 35.6cm). The right sides of the fabric should be facing each other inside the fold, and the wrong side should be facing out.

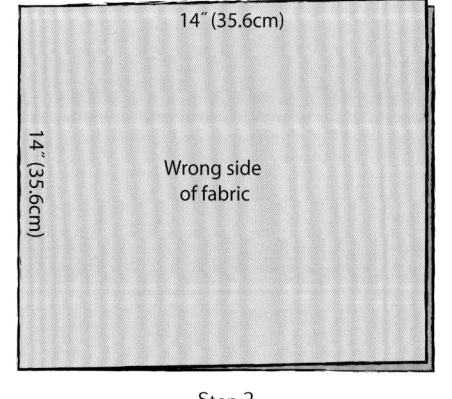

14″ (35.6cm)

14″ (35.6cm)

Wrong side of fabric

Step 2

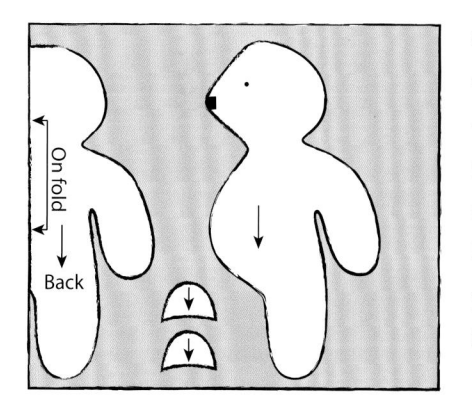

On fold

Back

Step 3: Pattern layout

3️⃣ Lay out the template pieces needed to make your chosen softie, following the layout shown. Remember to refer to the pattern marks to make sure the pieces are placed correctly. Each softie will need a back (cut on the fold) and 2 fronts (cut through both layers of fabric), and most will need 4 ear pieces (cut the shape twice through both layers of fabric—but watch for variations depending on the softie you're making). Make sure that the direction of pile arrows are all facing the same way.

4️⃣ Pin the template pieces securely through both layers of fabric. Step 5. Once the pieces are secured to the fabric, use a fabric pen to draw the outlines of the templates onto the fabric, and transfer the lettered pattern marks. Step 6. Cut the pieces out of both layers of fabric. Remove the template pieces and pins. You will have 1 back, 2 fronts, and 4 ears. Keep your fabric scraps, as they will be very useful for making small items like accessories or ears for another softie.

Fuzzy Ears

If you'd like, you can cut 2 of the 4 ear pieces from white short-pile faux fur fabric. This will make the inside of the ears look fuzzy!

Note

Once you feel more comfortable cutting out the pieces, you can just cut around the template and transfer the pattern marks instead of transferring the whole outline. But it's helpful to have the whole outline on the fabric.

STUFFING AND FINISHING THE SOFTIES

Stuffing

After you've finished sewing a softie, you'll need to fill it with polyester fiberfill. When you finish sewing, the softie will be inside out. Check all the seams to make sure there are no gaps, and then turn the softie right side out. Then it's time to grab the fiberfill.

Stuffing is simple, but follow these tips to make the process as smooth as possible:

- Add a small amount of fiberfill at a time, moving it into the correct place before adding more.

- Start at the extremities of the softie, like the tip of the nose and the ends of the paws. Then, fill the head, arms, shoulders, and legs. Last, fill the body cavity.

- Stuffing with your fingers is the easiest way to fill the softie, but if you're struggling to reach the smaller parts, a thick knitting needle or chopstick can help move the fiberfill around.

- Be gentle, and work slowly. You want to make sure that fiberfill reaches all parts of the softie, but you don't want any fiberfill to go through the seams.

- Don't overstuff the softie or stretch the fabric, or your softie might become misshapen.

- If the fiberfill looks lumpy, remove it and use your fingers to fluff it up.

- The overall shape of the softie should be symmetrical, so make sure you're not adding more fiberfill to one arm or leg than the other.

- Squeezing and shaping the fiberfill from the outside of the animal can also help adjust the shape to look more symmetrical. I often firmly squeeze the shoulder, neck, and arm areas to smooth the fiberfill.

Closing the Gap

When you are happy with the look and shape of your stuffed animal, it's time to close the gap (area marked **D** to **E** on all pattern pieces) where you inserted the stuffing. Close the gap with slip stitches (page 17).

Sewing the Eyes

After you figure out the unique eye placement noted in each project, you need to stitch the eyes on the softie. I recommend using eyes that are ¼″ (6mm) or bigger. Thread a long needle with black extra-strong thread.

Note

Remember that you can also sew eyes by embroidering black dots with satin stitches. This is a great option if you don't have time to shop for extra supplies, or if you're gifting the softie to a young child. Whenever you'll be sharing a softie with kids or babies, make sure the softie does not have any detachable parts or accessories.

1 Mark each eye position with a pin. While sewing on the eyes, we will call the eyes **A** and **B**.

At pin **A**, make a small double stitch. Then, insert the needle at **A** and bring it out at **B**. Pull the thread tight. The tension should be strong enough to make the fabric around **A** pucker and sink, like an eye socket. Double stitch at **B**.

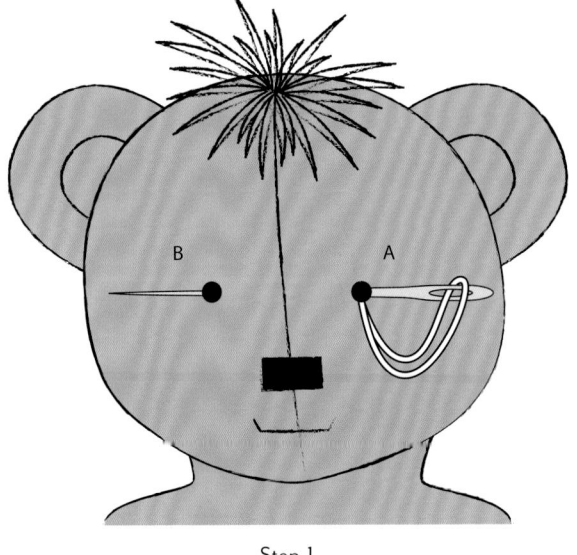

Step 1

Step 2

2 Thread a sew-in eye onto the needle and thread. Insert the needle at **B** and bring it out at **A**. After doing this, the first sew-in eye will be inserted at **B**. After exiting at **A**, keep the thread tight to pucker the eye socket at **B**. Double stitch at **A**.

3 Thread the second sew-in eye through the needle. Insert the needle at **A** and exit through the back of the softie's neck. Keep the tension tight and stitch a small double stitch on the neck to finish the eye sewing.

Step 3: A bow or collar will cover double stitches at back of neck.

Adding Color

I think adding rosy cheeks to the softies makes them look extra cute. Dip a pink or red watercolor pencil in water. Then, lightly dab the cheek area of your finished softie with the color. If you add too much, lift off excess color with a slightly damp cloth.

I recommend adding color after you've added the nose, mouth, eyes, and ears. Rosy cheeks look especially sweet when you're using plush felt.

Tummy Panels

Many of the softies, especially the fox, bear, and bunny, look great with a colored tummy panel. After finishing your softie, cut out a tummy panel (page 109) from a piece of fabric that complements the color of the softie. It's best to choose a fabric that does not fray.

Place the tummy panel on the softie's tummy, and then pin. Whipstitch (page 18) all the way around the panel to secure it to the softie. That's it! Get creative with fabric choices to fully take advantage of this feature.

Preparing to Sew

To recap, every simple softie project begins with the same three steps that we covered in this section:

1 Gather the necessary materials and select the pattern you'd like to make. See Fabrics and Materials (page 10).

2 Prepare your template pieces. See Pattern Pieces (page 22).

3 Lay out the templates, pin and mark your fabric, and then cut out the softie pieces. See Cutting the Fabric Pieces (page 23). Start with these three steps, and dive into the following projects to learn how to customize each adorable animal.

2

Animals

MCBEAR

Finished Size: 9˝ (23cm)

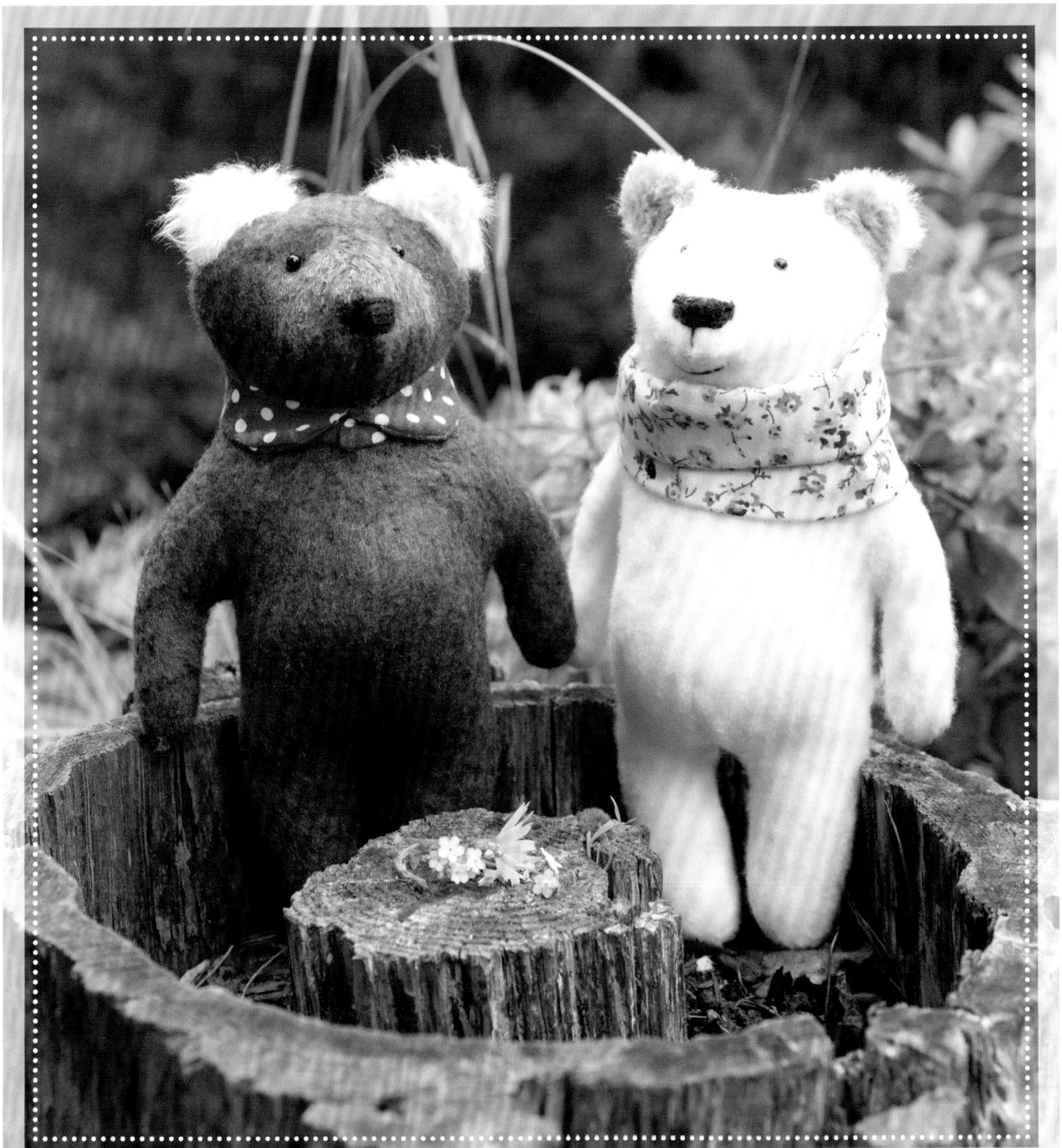

McBear is the most classic softie project. He's adorable and sweet in every way!

One note to keep in mind: McBear has a bit more challenging embroidered nose

than most of the other softies. You may choose to add a felt nose instead.

Materials

Plush felt or cuddle fleece: ½ yard (0.5m), or at least 14˝ × 24˝ (35.6 × 61cm)

White short-pile faux fur: 2˝ × 5˝ (5 × 12.7cm) for inner ears (optional)

Black felt: scrap for nose (optional)

Contrasting colored fabric: scrap for tummy panel (optional)

Sew-in eyes, ¼˝ (6mm): 2

All-purpose thread

Black embroidery thread

Black extra-strong thread

Polyester fiberfill

Standard hand-sewing needle

Large-eyed sewing needle

Long (about 3˝) sewing needle

Long sewing pins

Scissors

Water-erasable fabric pen

Pink or red watercolor pencil (optional)

After you've followed the steps in Preparing to Sew (page 27), it's time to start!

Cutting

Plush felt or cuddle fleece

Cut 1 back with Back.

Cut 2 fronts with Bear Front.

Cut 4 ears (2 if using optional faux fur) with Bear Ear.

Cut 1 tummy panel with Circle Tummy Panel (optional).

White faux fur (optional)

Cut 2 ears with Bear Ear.

Sewing McBear Together

All seam allowances are ¼˝ (6mm) unless otherwise noted.

STITCHES NEEDED FOR THIS PROJECT

Backstitch (page 16)

Slip stitch (page 17)

Satin stitch (page 19), optional

Whipstitch (page 18), optional

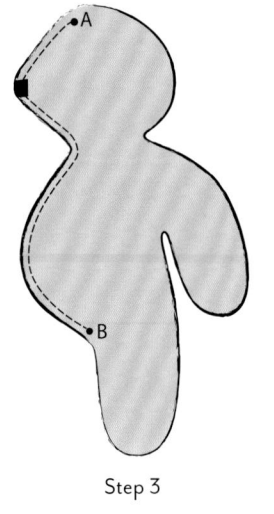

Step 3

1. Place 1 front fabric piece on top of the other with right sides together.

2. Pin the pieces together from dot **A** to dot **B** as marked from the pattern.

3. Thread the needle with all-purpose thread. Neatly sew with a ¼˝ (6mm) backstitch from dot **A** to dot **B**. You now have 1 front piece.

4. Lay the front piece flat with the right side facing up.

5. Place the back piece on top of the front piece with right sides together and McBear's arms and legs matching. Match the corresponding dots on both pieces, so that dot **A** on the back piece matches dot **A** on the front piece, and so forth for dots **B**, **C**, **D**, **E**, and **F**.

6. Securely pin the front and back pieces together.

7. Sew a ¼˝ (6mm) backstitch all the way around both pieces, with a ¼˝ (6mm) seam allowance, removing the pins as you go. Leave a gap between dot **D** and dot **E** in accordance with the pattern marks. Don't forget to add a double stitch to the start and end of the seam.

8. Check the stitching to ensure that there are no gaps.

9. Turn the softie right side out.

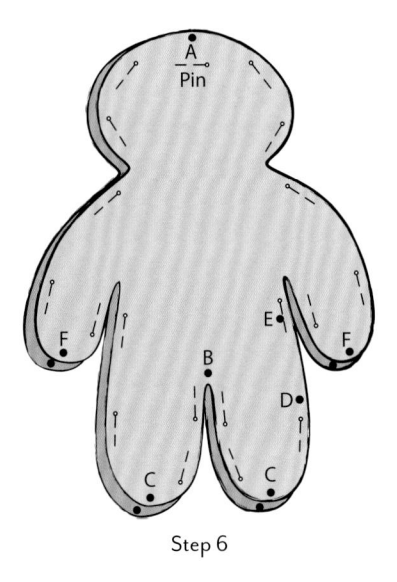

Step 6

Stuffing the Softie

Stuff McBear and then close the gap as outlined in Stuffing and Finishing the Softies (page 24). Slipstitch from dot **D** to dot **E**.

Adding the Face

Creating McBear's face is the most fun part of the process! Your little bear will come to life with just a few stitches. You can follow my guidelines to place the eyes, ears, and nose, or choose your own positioning to give your bear a unique personality.

McBear's Nose

To judge the nose position, turn McBear sideways and look at its profile. Plan to position the nose directly underneath the tip of the muzzle. ••••••••••••••••••••••••••••••➤

There are 2 options for attaching a nose, and 2 nose designs.

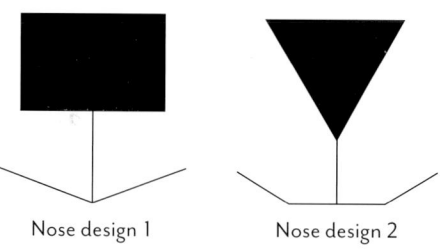

Nose design 1   Nose design 2

OPTION 1: FELT NOSE

To attach a felt nose to McBear, cut a square or triangle of black felt. Position it in the correct place and pin. Then, attach it to the face by sewing all the way around the nose with a small slip stitch.

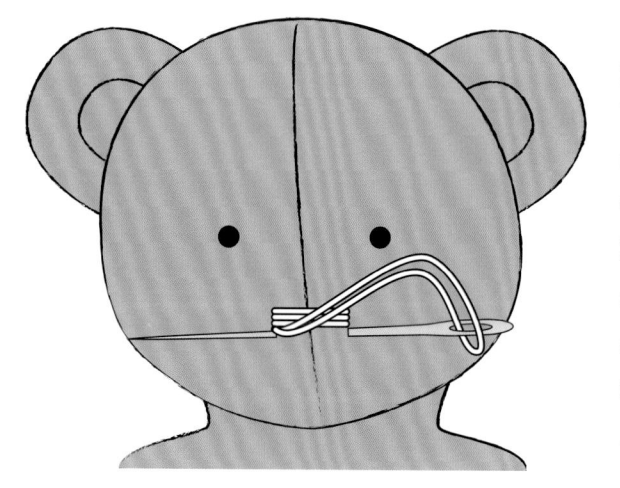

OPTION 2: STITCHED NOSE

To stitch the nose onto McBear, thread the large-eye needle with black embroidery thread. Mark a few dots on McBear's face with the fabric pen to indicate where you would like the nose to be positioned.

Use a satin stitch to fill in the nose shape. Make sure the stitches are flat and flush to the face, but don't pull the thread too tight, or the nose will start to look puckered.

◄•••••••••••••••••••••••••••••••••

McBear's Mouth

After sewing the nose, refer again to the 2 nose design options. It's time to sew a few stitches for the mouth to match one of the designs, using the large-eyed needle and black embroidery thread.

1 At the bottom right corner of the nose, insert the needle at point **A** and bring it out at point **B**, aligned under the middle of the nose (or the bottom point of the triangle nose).

2 Stitch from **B** to **C**. Then, bring the needle up through the fabric at point **D**. Backstitch back to point **C**.

3 Repeat on the other side at point **E**, backstitching back to point **C**.

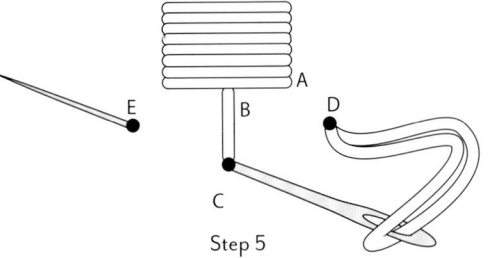

Step 5

4 Optional: Adjust your stitches to make the mouth in nose design 2.

5 Bring the needle all the way through the softie and out at the back of the neck. Double stitch to hold the thread in place.

Seams

In order to correctly position the eyes and ears, we're going to refer to the seams on McBear. Note the following seams on your softie:

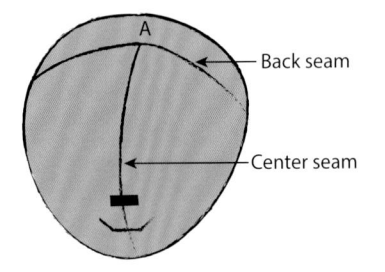

- ♥ CENTER SEAM: seam down the middle of the head where the 2 front pieces are sewn together

- ♥ BACK SEAM: seam across the top of the head where the back and front of the head are sewn together

- ♥ POINT **A**: spot where the center seam and back seam meet in the middle of the head

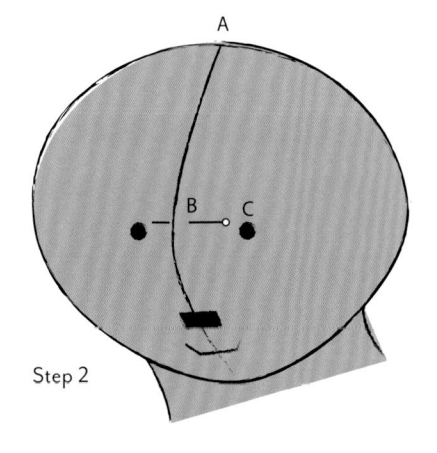

Step 2

Placing and Sewing McBear's Eyes

1 Identify point **A** on the top of the softie's head. Measure 1½˝ (3.8cm) from point **A** along the center seam and add a pin to mark point **B**.

2 Measure 1˝ (2.5cm) to the left and right of point **B** to identify the placement of each eye (point **C**). Mark each eye with a dot or pin, and then remove the pin for point **B**. Look at your softie to make sure the eyes are level and evenly spaced from the center seam.

3 Follow the instructions in Sewing the Eyes (page 25) to sew or embroider the eyes onto McBear.

Placing and Sewing McBear's Ears

1 Divide the 4 ear pieces into pairs. Place them right sides together; then backstitch around the curved part of each ear, leaving the straight edge open. Don't forget to double stitch at the beginning and end!

2 Turn the ears right side out.

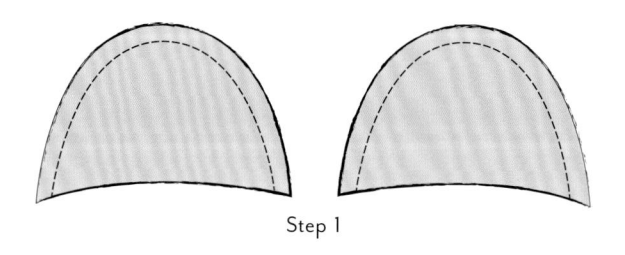

Step 1

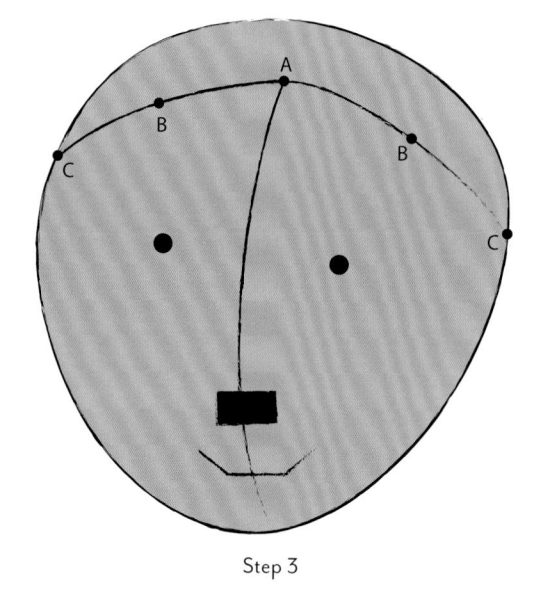

Step 3

3 Identify point **A** on the top of the softie's head. Measure 1˝ (2.5cm) from point **A** to the left and right along the back seam and add a pin on each side, creating 2 points **B**.

4 Measure 1˝ (2.5cm) past each point **B** along the back seam and mark with a pin to create each point **C**. Point **C** is the outer edge of the ear.

5 Pin each ear to the head from points **B** to **C**. Make sure that the ears are level and at the same height. They should both be along the back seam.

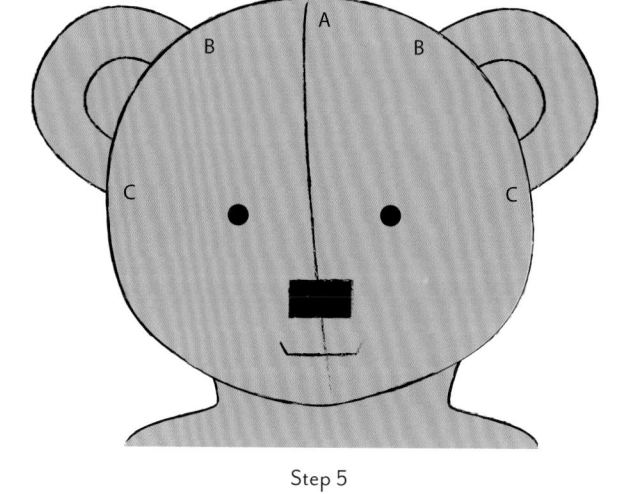

Step 5

Teddy Bear Softie: McBear

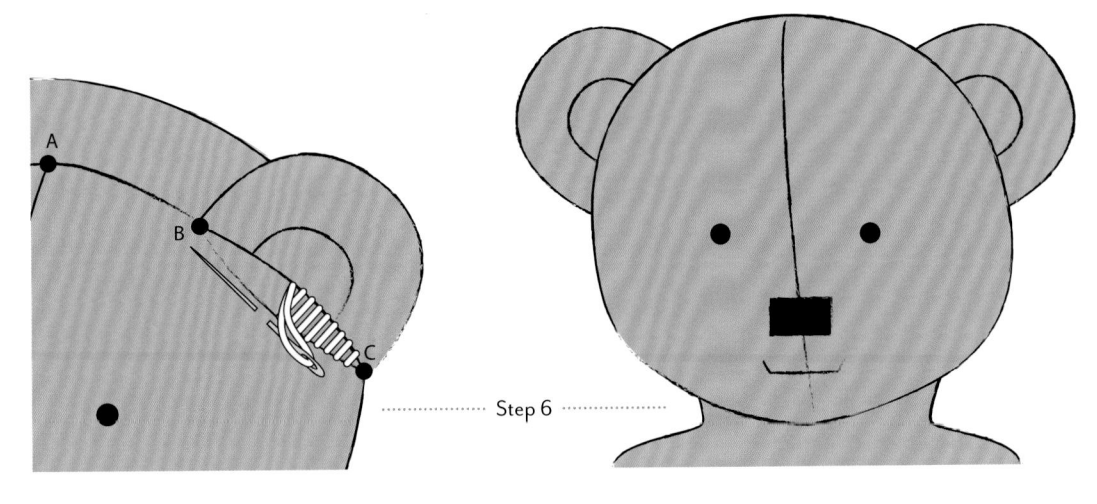

························ Step 6 ························

6 Slipstitch each ear to the head, using small stitches.

If you'd like to add a tummy panel to your bear, follow the instructions in Tummy Panels (page 27).

Tip

If you created your softie with dark-colored fabric, the mouth and nose might not stand out enough. To remedy this, water down some white or light-colored acrylic paint. Dab the nose and muzzle area with the paint until they have lightened up enough for the nose and mouth to stand out. Paint a little at a time, brushing in the direction of the pile. Let the paint dry before adding more, building it up until you are happy with the color. If there is too much paint on the muzzle, remove excess with a damp cloth.

Paw Marks

Embroidered paw marks are an adorable finishing touch for McBear.

Add color to McBear's cheeks if you'd like, using a pink or red watercolor pencil (see Adding Color, page 27); check all the seams and facial features to make sure they're secure; and evenly distribute the fiberfill if any lumps have developed. McBear is ready!

Using embroidery thread, stitch 3 short lines along edge of each paw.

Teddy Bear Softie: McBear

NELLYPHANT

Finished Size: 9˝ (23cm)

Nellyphant has a big personality, with large ears and a long trunk. Because of the trunk, there's no nose to place.

After you've followed the steps in Preparing to Sew (page 27), it's time to start!

Materials

Plush felt or cuddle fleece: ½ yard (0.5m), or at least 14˝ × 24˝ (35.6 × 61cm)

White short-pile faux fur: 5˝ × 9˝ (12.7 × 22.9cm) for inner ears (optional)

Sew-in eyes, ¼˝ (6mm): 2

All-purpose thread

Black embroidery thread

Black extra-strong thread

Polyester fiberfill

Standard hand-sewing needle

Large-eyed sewing needle

Long (about 3˝) sewing needle

Long sewing pins

Scissors

Water-erasable fabric pen

Pink or red watercolor pencil (optional)

Cutting

Plush felt or cuddle fleece

Cut 1 back with Back.

Cut 2 fronts with Elephant Front.

Cut 4 ears (2 if using optional faux fur) with Elephant Ear.

White faux fur (optional)

Cut 2 ears with Elephant Ear.

Sewing Nellyphant Together

All seam allowances are ¼″ (6mm) unless otherwise noted.

STITCHES NEEDED FOR THIS PROJECT

Backstitch (page 16)

Slip stitch (page 17)

Satin stitch (page 19), optional

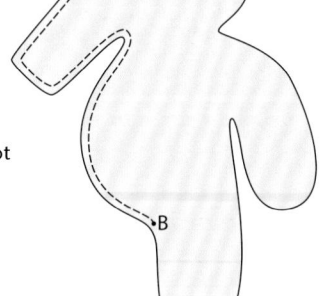

Step 3

1️⃣ Place 1 front fabric piece on top of the other with right sides together.

2️⃣ Pin the pieces together from dot **A** to dot **B** as marked from the pattern.

3️⃣ Thread the needle with all-purpose thread. Neatly sew with a ¼″ (6mm) backstitch from dot **A** to dot **B**. You now have 1 front piece.

4️⃣ Lay the front piece flat with the right side facing up.

5️⃣ Place the back piece on top of the front piece with right sides together and Nellyphant's arms and legs matching. Match the corresponding dots on both pieces, so that dot **A** on the back piece matches dot **A** on the front piece, and so forth for dots **B**, **C**, **D**, **E**, and **F**.

6️⃣ Securely pin the front and back pieces together.

7️⃣ Sew a ¼″ (6mm) backstitch all the way around both pieces with a ¼″ (6mm) seam allowance, removing the pins as you go. Leave a gap between dot **D** and dot **E** in accordance with the pattern marks. Don't forget to add a double stitch to the start and end of the seam.

8️⃣ Check the stitching to ensure that there are no gaps.

9️⃣ Turn the softie right side out.

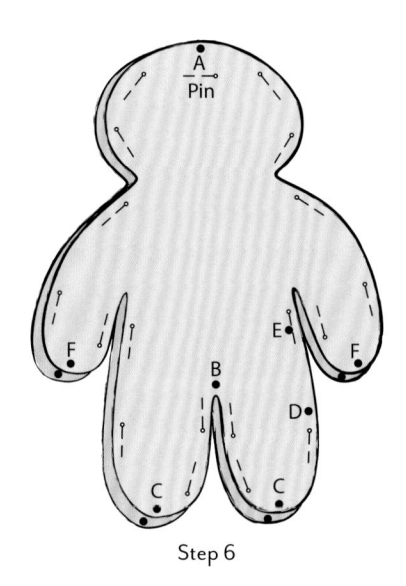

Step 6

Stuffing the Softie

Stuff Nellyphant as outlined in Stuffing and Finishing the Softies (page 24). Be extra careful stuffing Nellyphant's trunk! Close the gap you used to insert the stuffing. Slipstitch from dot **D** to dot **E**.

Adding the Face

Creating Nellyphant's face lets you add a lot of personality. You can follow my guidelines to place the eyes and ears, or choose your own positioning to make your softie unique.

Seams

In order to correctly position the eyes and ears, we're going to refer to the seams on Nellyphant. Note the following seams on your softie:

- CENTER SEAM: seam down the middle of the head where the 2 front pieces are sewn together

- BACK SEAM: seam across the top of the head where the back and front of the head are sewn together

- POINT **A**: spot where the center seam and back seam meet in the middle of the head

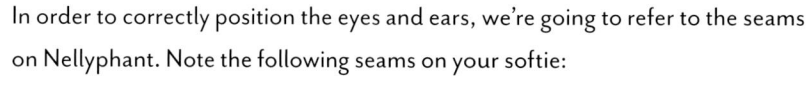

Placing and Sewing Nellyphant's Eyes

1 Identify point **A** on the top of the softie's head. Measure 1½˝ (3.8cm) from point **A** along the center seam and add a pin to mark point **B**.

2 Measure 1˝ (2.5cm) to the left and right of point **B** to identify the placement of each eye (point **C**). Mark each eye with a dot or pin, and then remove the pin for point **B**. Look at your softie to make sure the pins are level and evenly spaced from the center seam.

3 Follow the instructions in Sewing the Eyes (page 25) to sew or embroider the eyes onto Nellyphant.

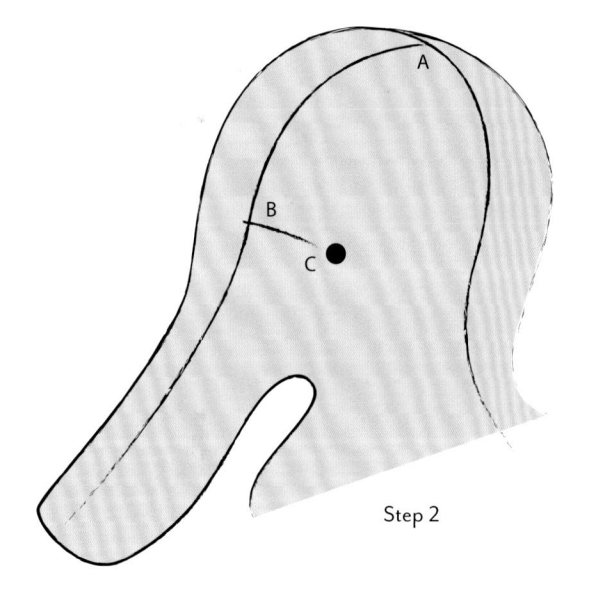

Step 2

Placing and Sewing Nellyphant's Ears

There are 2 possible positions for the elephant ears: horizontal or vertical placement.

1 Divide the 4 ear pieces into pairs. Place them right sides together; then backstitch around the curved part of each ear, leaving the straight edge open. Don't forget to double stitch at the beginning and end!

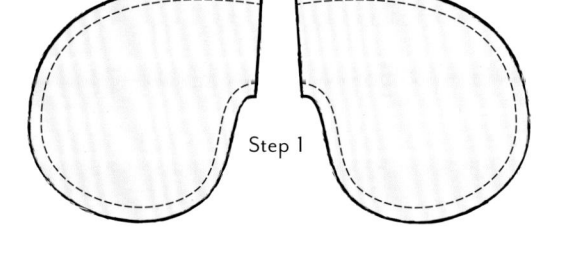

Step 1

2 Turn the ears right side out. Fold in the raw edges of the unsewn straight edge; then sew together using small slip stitches to close the ears.

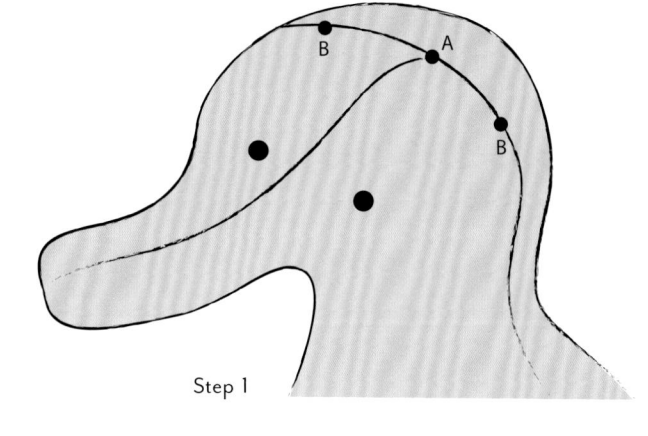

Step 1

HORIZONTAL PLACEMENT

1 When the ears are placed horizontally, the curve of each ear faces forward. Identify point **A** on the top of the softie's head. Measure 1⅝˝ (4.1cm) from point **A** to the left and right along the back seam and add a pin on each side, creating 2 points **B**.

2 Match point **X** on the ear to point **B** on the back seam. Pin the ear to the head, keeping the top edge horizontal. Slipstitch each ear to the head using small stitches.

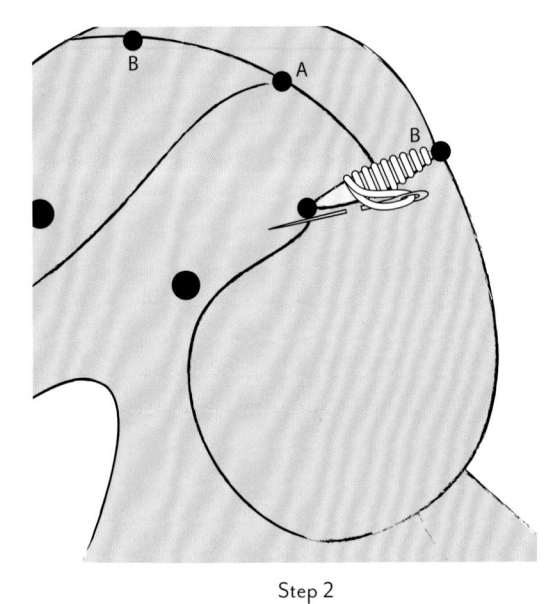

Step 2

VERTICAL EAR PLACEMENT

If you prefer the ears to stand out to the side of the head, sew them vertically instead.

1 Measure 1⅝˝ (4.1cm) from each point **B** along the back seam downward and add a pin to create point **C**. Point **C** is the bottom edge of the ear.

2 Pin each ear to the head from point **B** to point **C**, with the curve of each ear facing down. Make sure that the ears are level and at the same height. They should both be along the back seam. Slipstitch each ear to the head using small stitches.

Add color to Nellyphant's cheeks if you'd like, using a pink or red watercolor pencil (see Adding Color, page 27); check all the seams and facial features to make sure they're secure; and evenly distribute the fiberfill if any lumps have developed. Nellyphant is ready!

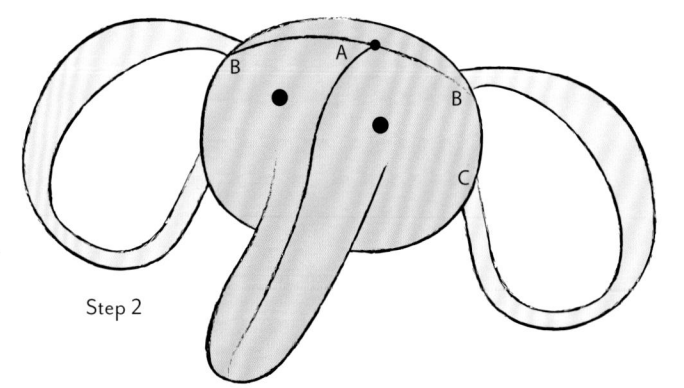

Step 2

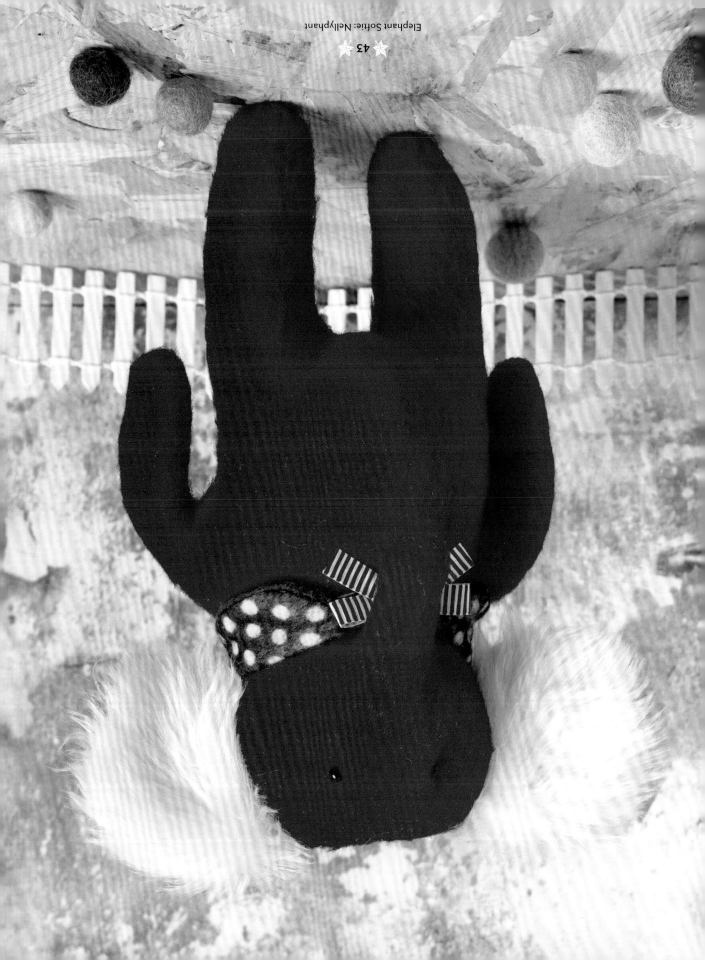

MOUSE SOFTIE

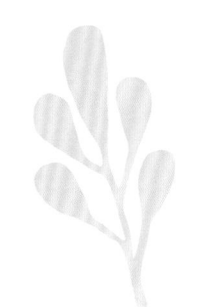

LITTLE MOUSE

Finished Size: 9˝ (23cm)

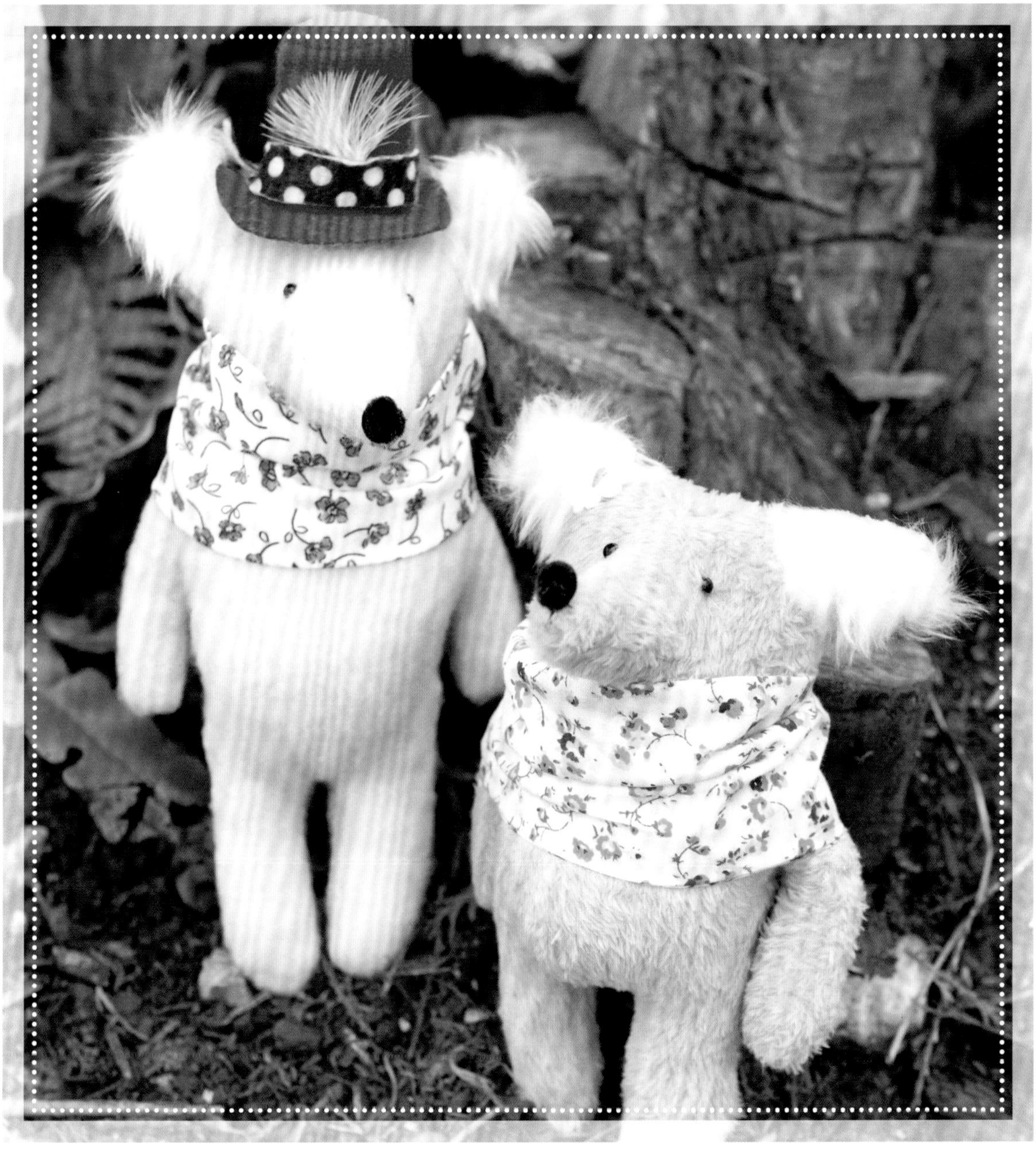

Little Mouse is so cute and curious! Making Little Mouse is very similar to making McBear.

After you've followed the steps in Preparing to Sew (page 27), it's time to start!

Materials

Plush felt or cuddle fleece: ½ yard (0.5m), or at least 14˝ × 24˝ (35.6 × 61cm)

White short-pile faux fur: 3˝ × 4˝ (7.6 × 10.2cm) for inner ears (optional)

Sew-in eyes, ¼˝ (6mm): 2

Pom-pom, ³⁄₈˝ (10mm), black: 1 for nose (optional)

All-purpose thread

Black embroidery thread

Black extra-strong thread

Polyester fiberfill

Standard hand-sewing needle

Large-eyed sewing needle

Long (about 3˝) sewing needle

Long sewing pins

Scissors

Water-erasable fabric pen

Pink or red watercolor pencil (optional)

Cutting

Plush felt or cuddle fleece

Cut 1 back with Back.

Cut 2 fronts with Mouse Front.

Cut 4 ears (2 if using optional faux fur) with Mouse Ear.

White faux fur (optional)

Cut 2 ears with Mouse Ear.

Sewing Little Mouse Together

All seam allowances are ¼˝ (6mm) unless otherwise noted.

STITCHES NEEDED FOR THIS PROJECT

Backstitch (page 16)

Slip stitch (page 17)

Satin stitch (page 19), optional

1 Place 1 front fabric piece on top of the other with right sides together.

2 Pin the pieces together from dot **A** to dot **B** as marked from the pattern.

3 Thread the needle with all purpose thread. Neatly sew with a ¼˝ (6mm) backstitch from dot **A** to dot **B**. You now have 1 front piece.

4 Lay the front piece flat with the right side facing up.

Step 3

5 Place the back piece on top of the front piece with right sides together and Little Mouse's arms and legs matching. Match the corresponding dots on both pieces, so that dot **A** on the back piece matches dot **A** on the front piece, and so forth for dots **B**, **C**, **D**, **E**, and **F**.

6 Securely pin the front and back pieces together.

7 Sew a ¼˝ (6mm) backstitch all the way around both pieces, with a ¼˝ (6mm) seam allowance, removing the pins as you go. Leave a gap between dot **D** and dot **E** in accordance with the pattern marks. Don't forget to add a double stitch to the start and end of the seam.

8 Check the stitching to ensure that there are no gaps.

9 Turn the softie right side out.

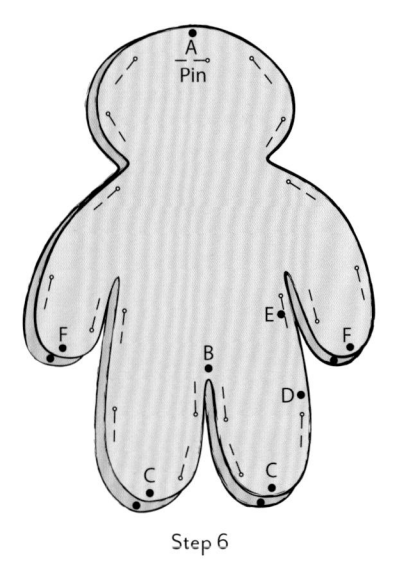

Step 6

Stuffing the Softie

Stuff Little Mouse and close the gap as outlined in Stuffing and Finishing the Softies (page 24). Slipstitch from dot **D** to dot **E**.

Adding the Face

Creating Little Mouse's face is fun and easy! You can follow my guidelines to place the eyes, ears, and nose, or choose your own positioning to give your mouse a unique personality.

Little Mouse's Nose

To judge the nose position, turn Little Mouse sideways and look at its profile. Directly at the end of the long, pointy snout, attach the ⅜″ (10mm) black pom-pom with a dot of glue, or use satin stitch to sew a round nose in black embroidery thread.

Seams

In order to correctly position the eyes and ears, we're going to refer to the seams on Little Mouse. Note the following seams on your softie:

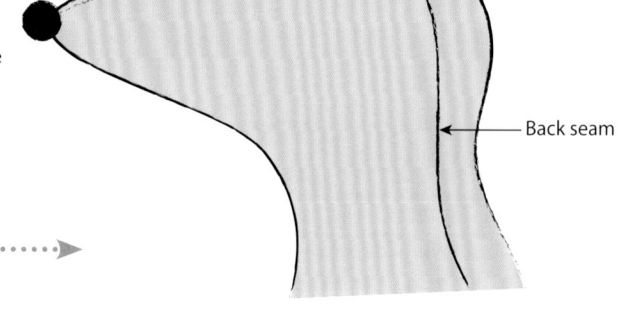

- ♥ Center seam: seam down the middle of the head where the 2 front pieces are sewn together

- ♥ Back seam: seam across the top of the head where the back and front of the head are sewn together

- ♥ Point **A**: spot where the center seam and back seam meet in the middle of the head

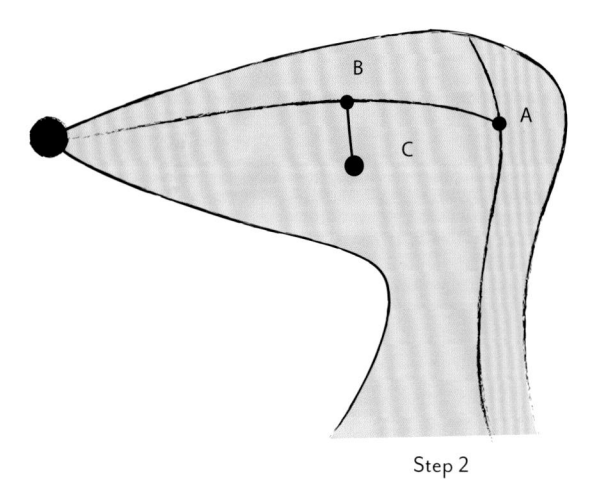

Step 2

Placing and Sewing Little Mouse's Eyes

1 Identify point **A** on the top of the softie's head. Measure 1½″ (3.8cm) from point **A** along the center seam and add a pin to mark point **B**.

2 Measure 1¼″ (3.2cm) to the left and right of point **B** to identify the placement of each eye (point **C**). Mark each eye with a dot or pin, and then remove the pin for point **B**. Look at your softie to make sure the eyes are level and evenly spaced from the center seam.

3 Follow the instructions in Sewing the Eyes (page 25) to sew or embroider the eyes onto Little Mouse.

Placing and Sewing Little Mouse's Ears

1 Divide the 4 ear pieces into pairs. Place them right sides together; then backstitch around the curved part of each ear, leaving the straight edge open. Don't forget to double stitch at the beginning and end!

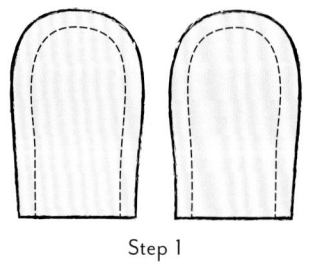

Step 1

2 Turn the ears right side out.

3 Identify point **A** on the top of the softie's head. Measure 1˝ (2.5cm) from point **A** to the left and right along the back seam and add a pin on each side, creating 2 points **B**.

4 Measure 1˝ (2.5cm) past each point **B** along the back seam and mark with a pin to create each point **C**. Point **C** is the outer edge of the ear.

5 There are 2 ways to attach Little Mouse's ears:

Pin each ear between point **B** and point **C**, with both ears facing either back or up. Make sure that the ears are level and at the same height. They should both be along the back seam.

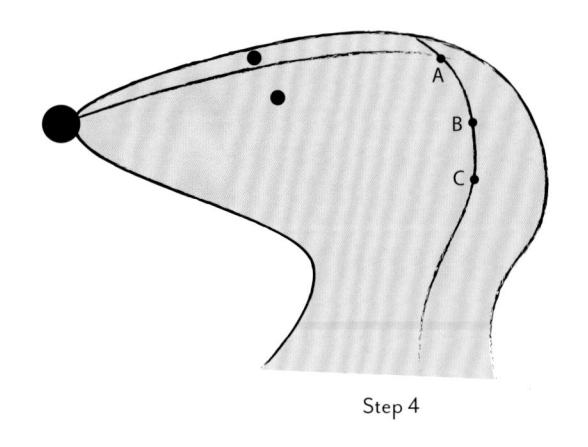

Step 4

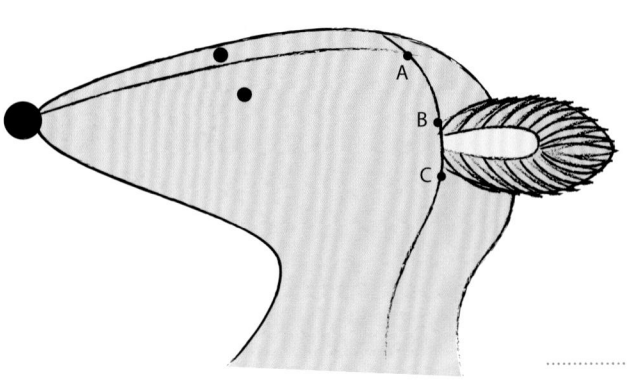

Ears pointing back

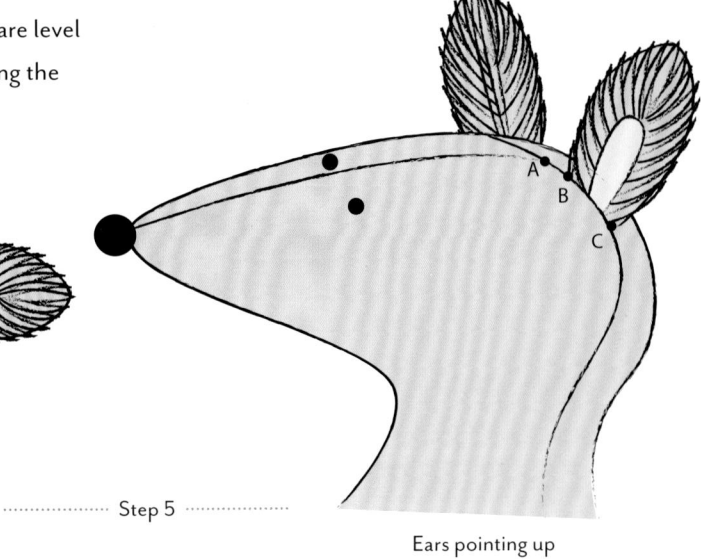

Step 5

Ears pointing up

Step 6

6 Slipstitch each ear to the head, using small stitches.

Add color to Little Mouse's cheeks if you'd like, using a pink or red watercolor pencil (see Adding Color, page 27); check all the seams and facial features to make sure they're secure; and evenly distribute the fiberfill if any lumps have developed. Little Mouse is ready!

FOX SOFTIE
FAB FOXY

Finished Size: 9~ (23cm)

Fab Foxy is a cunning and cute softie! I love adding a white tummy to make Fab Foxy more dashing. Fab Foxy's ears sit tall and upright, so they need a little bit of extra care. Some fabrics are too soft and won't stay up. So, sometimes I like to use stiff felt for the ears. If you're using stiff felt, you only need to cut 2 ear pieces.

Materials

Plush felt or cuddle fleece: ½ yard (0.5m), or at least 14˝ × 24˝ (35.6 × 61cm)

Stiff felt: 4˝ × 8˝ (10.2 × 20.3cm) for ears (optional)

White short-pile faux fur: 8˝ × 9˝ (20.3 × 22.9cm) for inner ears and tummy panel (optional)

Sew-in eyes, ¼˝ (6mm): 2

Pom-pom, ⅜˝ (10mm), black: 1 for nose (optional)

All-purpose thread

Black embroidery thread

Black extra-strong thread

Polyester fiberfill

Standard hand-sewing needle

Large-eyed sewing needle

Long (about 3˝) sewing needle

Long sewing pins

Scissors

Water-erasable fabric pen

Pink or red watercolor pencil (optional)

After you've followed the steps in Preparing to Sew (page 27), it's time to start!

Cutting

Plush felt or cuddle fleece

Cut 1 back with Back.

Cut 2 fronts with Fox Front.

Cut 4 ears (2 if using optional faux fur, or none if using optional stiff felt) with Fox Ear.

Stiff felt (optional)

Cut 2 ears with Fox Ear.

White faux fur (optional)

Cut 2 ears with Fox Ear.

Cut 1 tummy panel with Tummy Panel.

Sewing Fab Foxy Together

All seam allowances are ¼˝ (6mm) unless otherwise noted.

STITCHES NEEDED FOR THIS PROJECT

Backstitch (page 16)

Slip stitch (page 17)

Satin stitch (page 19), optional

Whipstitch (page 18), optional

1 Place 1 front fabric piece on top of the other with right sides together.

2 Pin the pieces together from dot **A** to dot **B** as marked from the pattern.

3 Thread the needle with all-purpose thread. Neatly sew with a ¼˝ (6mm) backstitch from dot **A** to dot **B**. You now have 1 front piece.

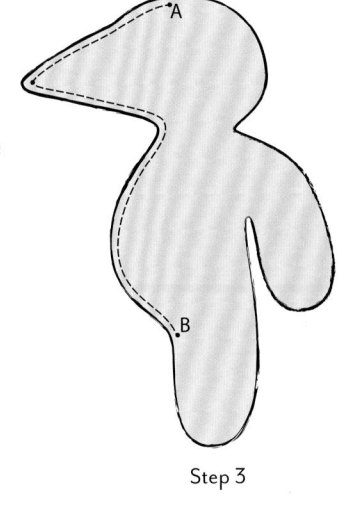

Step 3

4 Lay the front piece flat with the right side facing up.

5 Place the back piece on top of the front piece with right sides together and Fab Foxy's arms and legs matching. Match the corresponding dots on both pieces, so that dot **A** on the back piece matches dot **A** on the front piece, and so forth for dots **B**, **C**, **D**, **E**, and **F**.

6 Securely pin the front and back pieces together.

7 Sew a ¼˝ (6mm) backstitch all the way around both pieces, with a ¼˝ (6mm) seam allowance, removing the pins as you go. Leave a gap between dot **D** and dot **E** in accordance with the pattern marks. Don't forget to add a double stitch to the start and end of the seam.

8 Check the stitching to ensure that there are no gaps.

9 Turn the softie right side out.

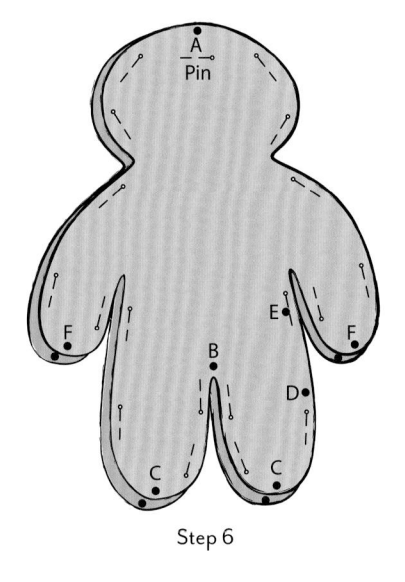

Step 6

Stuffing the Softie

Stuff Fab Foxy and close the gap as outlined in Stuffing and Finishing the Softies (page 24). Slipstitch from dot **D** to dot **E**.

Adding the Face

Creating Fab Foxy's face adds a world of personality! You can follow my guidelines to place the eyes, ears, and nose, or choose your own positioning to give your fox a unique personality.

Fab Foxy's Nose

To judge the nose position, turn Fab Foxy sideways and look at its profile. Directly at the end of the long, pointy snout, attach the ⅜″ (10mm) black pom-pom with a dot of glue, or use satin stitch to sew a round nose in black embroidery thread.

Seams

In order to correctly position the eyes and ears, we're going to refer to the seams on Fab Foxy. Note the following seams on your softie:

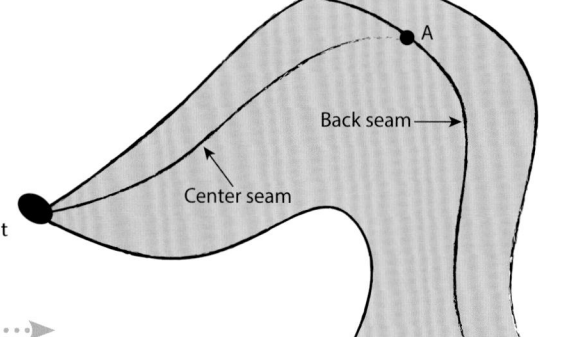

- ♥ Center seam: seam down the middle of the head where the 2 front pieces are sewn together

- ♥ Back seam: seam across the top of the head where the back and front of the head are sewn together

- ♥ Point **A**: spot where the center seam and back seam meet in the middle of the head

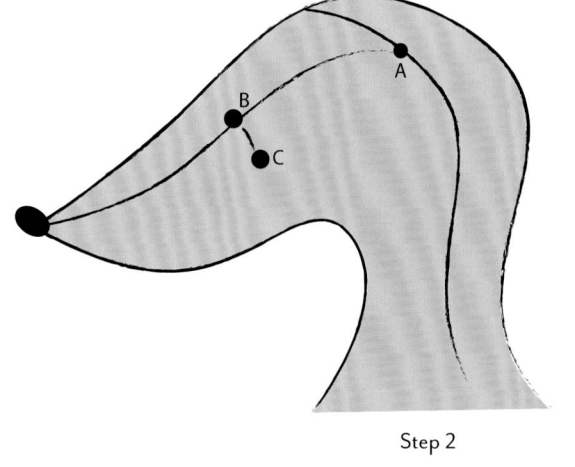

Step 2

Placing and Sewing Fab Foxy's Eyes

1 Identify point **A** on the top of the softie's head. Measure 1½″ (3.8cm) from point **A** along the center seam and add a pin to mark point **B**.

2 Measure 1″ (2.5cm) to the left and right of point **B** to identify the placement of each eye (point **C**). Mark each eye with a dot or pin, and then remove the pin for point **B**. Look at your softie to make sure the eyes are level and evenly spaced from the center seam.

3 Follow the instructions in Sewing the Eyes (page 25) to sew or embroider the eyes onto Fab Foxy.

Placing and Sewing Fab Foxy's Ears

If you're using stiff felt you will have only 2 ear pieces. Skip Steps 1 and 2.

1 Divide the 4 ear pieces into pairs. Place them right sides together; then backstitch around the pointed part of each ear, leaving the straight edge open. Don't forget to double stitch at the beginning and end!

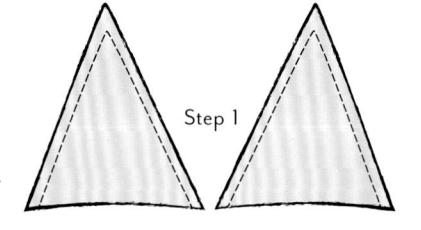

Step 1

2 Turn the ears right side out. If you are using a fabric that does not fray, you can also leave the ears with the wrong sides facing out and the stitches showing for a new look.

3 Identify point **A** on the top of the softie's head. Measure 2″ (5.1cm) from point **A** to the left and right along the back seam and add a pin on each side, creating 2 points **B**.

4 Fold the ear along the fold line marked on the pattern. The X marks the midpoint on the folded ear along the straight edge.

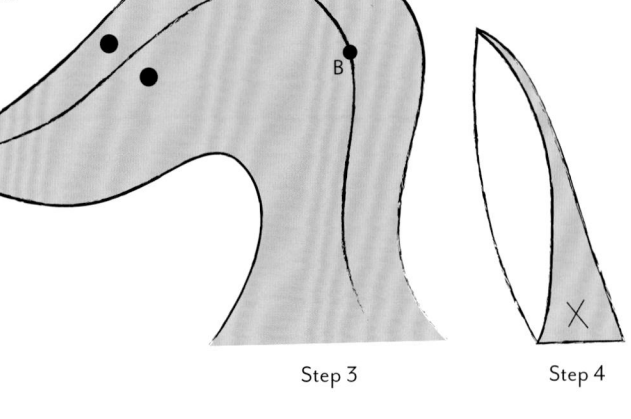

Step 3   Step 4

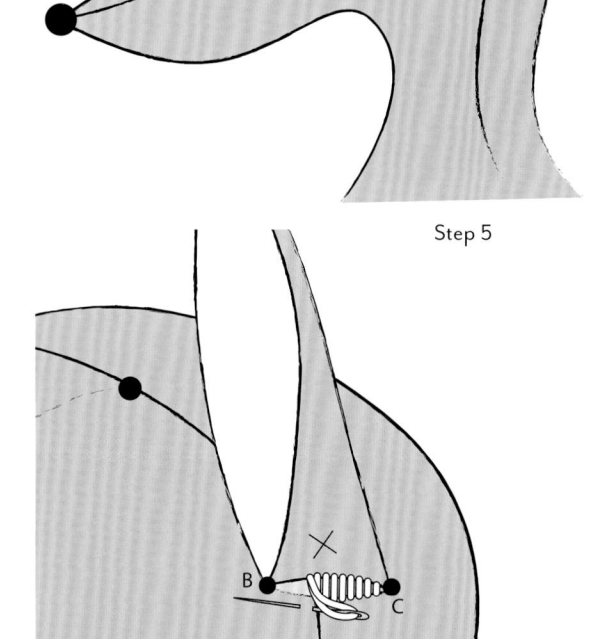

Step 5

5 Match the **X** on the ear to point **B** on the back seam and pin the ears to the head, pointing them straight up. Make sure that the ears are level and at the same height.

6 Slipstitch each ear to the head using small stitches.

If you'd like to add a white tummy panel to your fox, follow the instructions in Tummy Panels (page 27).

Add color to Foxy's cheeks if you'd like, using a pink or red watercolor pencil (see Adding Color, page 27); check all the seams and facial features to make sure they're secure; and evenly distribute the fiberfill if any lumps have developed. Fab Foxy is ready!

Step 6

Fox Softie: Fab Foxie

WOOFY

Finished Size: 9˝ (23cm)

Woofy is the perfect companion! With cute floppy ears and a long snout, this adorable dog softie will make everyone smile. For an exciting variation, cut Woofy's ears from a different-colored fabric!

After you've followed the steps in Preparing to Sew (page 27), it's time to start!

Materials

Plush felt or cuddle fleece: ½ yard (0.5m), or at least 14˝ × 24˝ (35.6 × 61cm)

Contrasting plush felt, fleece, or short-pile faux fur: 7˝ × 10˝ (17.8 × 25.4cm) for ears (optional)

Pom-pom, ⅜˝ (10mm), black: 1 for nose (optional)

Sew-in eyes, ¼˝ (6mm): 2

All-purpose thread

Black embroidery thread

Black extra-strong thread

Polyester fiberfill

Standard hand-sewing needle

Large-eyed sewing needle

Long (about 3˝) sewing needle

Long sewing pins

Scissors

Water-erasable fabric pen

Pink or red watercolor pencil (optional)

Cutting

Plush felt or cuddle fleece

Cut 1 back with Back.

Cut 2 fronts with Dog Front.

Cut 4 ears with Dog Ear (or none if using optional contrasting fabric).

Contrasting plush felt, fleece, or faux fur (optional)

Cut 4 ears with Dog Ear.

Sewing Woofy Together

All seam allowances are ¼˝ (6mm) unless otherwise noted.

STITCHES NEEDED FOR THIS PROJECT

Backstitch (page 16)

Slip stitch (page 17)

Satin stitch (page 19), optional

1 Place 1 front fabric piece on top of the other with right sides together.

2 Pin the pieces together from dot **A** to dot **B** as marked from the pattern.

3 Thread the needle with all-purpose thread. Neatly sew with a ¼˝ (6mm) backstitch from dot **A** to dot **B**. You now have 1 front piece.

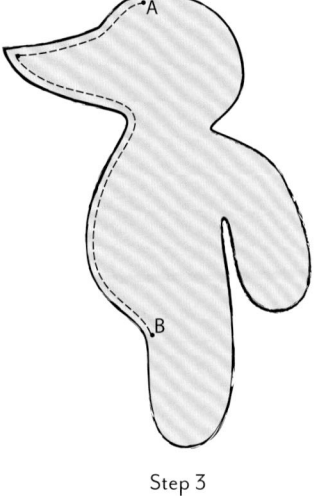

Step 3

4 Lay the front piece flat with the right side facing up.

5 Place the back piece on top of the front piece with right sides together and Woofy's arms and legs matching. Match the corresponding dots on both pieces, so that dot **A** on the back piece matches dot **A** on the front piece, and so forth for dots **B**, **C**, **D**, **E**, and **F**.

6 Securely pin the front and back pieces together.

7 Sew a ¼˝ (6mm) backstitch all the way around both pieces, with a ¼˝ (6mm) seam allowance, removing the pins as you go. Leave a gap between dot **D** and dot **E** in accordance with the pattern marks. Don't forget to add a double stitch to the start and end of the seam.

8 Check the stitching to ensure that there are no gaps.

9 Turn the softie right side out.

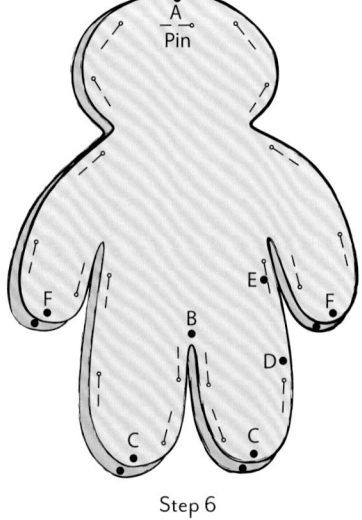

Step 6

Stuffing the Softie

Stuff Woofy and close the gap as outlined in Stuffing and Finishing the Softies (page 24). Slipstitch from dot **D** to dot **E**.

Adding the Face

Creating Woofy's face adds personality! You can follow my guidelines to place the eyes, ears, and nose, or choose your own positioning to make your dog stand out.

Woofy's Nose

To judge the nose position, turn Woofy sideways and look at its profile. Directly at the end of the long, pointy snout, attach the ⅜˝ (10mm) black pom-pom with a dot of glue, or use satin stitch to sew a round nose in black embroidery thread.

Seams

In order to correctly position the eyes and ears, we're going to refer to the seams on Woofy. Note the following seams on your softie:

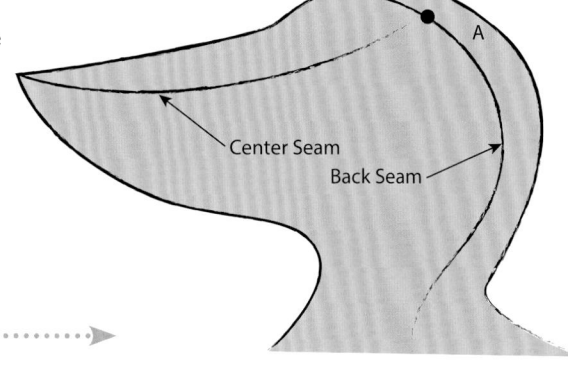

- Center seam: seam down the middle of the head where the 2 front pieces are sewn together

- Back seam: seam across the top of the head where the back and front of the head are sewn together

- Point **A**: spot where the center seam and back seam meet in the middle of the head

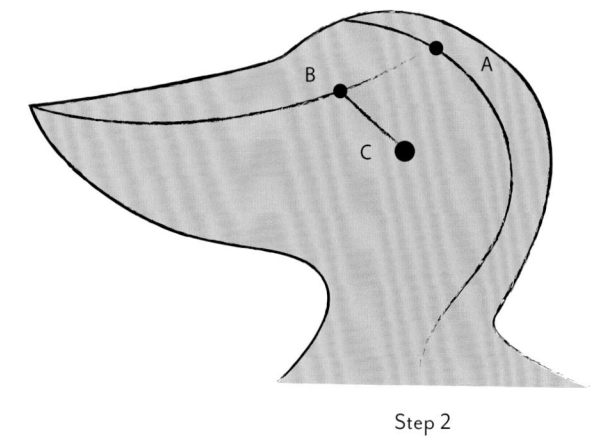

Step 2

Placing and Sewing Woofy's Eyes

1 Identify point **A** on the top of the softie's head. Measure 1¼˝ (3.2cm) from point **A** along the center seam and add a pin to mark point **B**.

2 Measure 1˝ (2.5cm) to the left and right of point **B** to identify the placement of each eye (point **C**). Mark each eye with a dot or pin, and then remove the pin for point **B**. Look at your softie to make sure the eyes are level and evenly spaced from the center seam.

3 Follow the instructions in Sewing the Eyes (page 25) to sew or embroider the eyes onto Woofy.

Placing and Sewing Woofy's Ears

1 Divide the 4 ear pieces into pairs. Place them right sides together; then backstitch around the curved part of each ear, leaving the straight edge open. Don't forget to double stitch at the beginning and end!

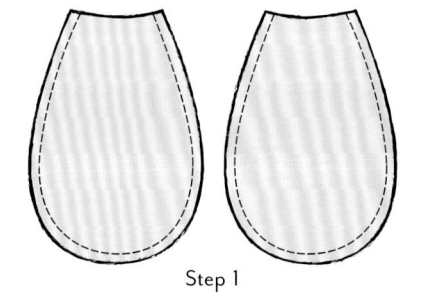

Step 1

2 Turn the ears right side out. Fold in the raw edges of the unsewn straight edge; then sew together using small slip stitches.

3 Identify point **A** on the top of the softie's head. Measure 2″ (5.1cm) from point **A** to the left and right along the back seam and add a pin on each side, creating 2 points **B**.

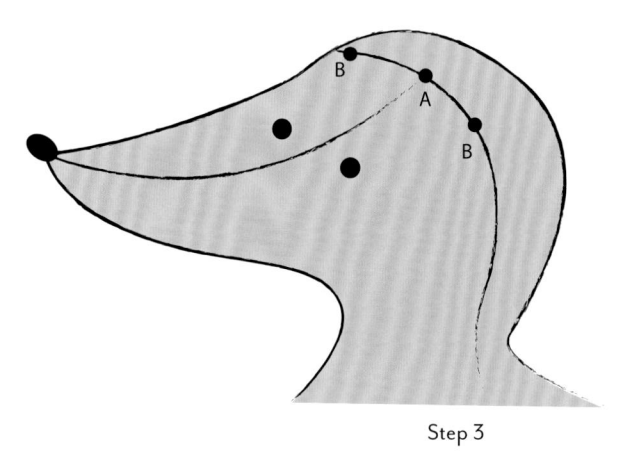

Step 3

4 Point **X** is the midpoint on the straight edge of the ear. Match the **X** on the ear to point **B** on the back seam, keeping the top edge of the ear horizontal.

5 Pin each ear to the head at point **B**. Make sure that the ears are level and at the same height.

6 Slipstitch each ear to the head using small stitches.

Add color to Woofy's cheeks if you'd like, using a pink or red watercolor pencil (see Adding Color, page 27); check all the seams and facial features to make sure they're secure; and evenly distribute the fiberfill if any lumps have developed. Woofy is ready!

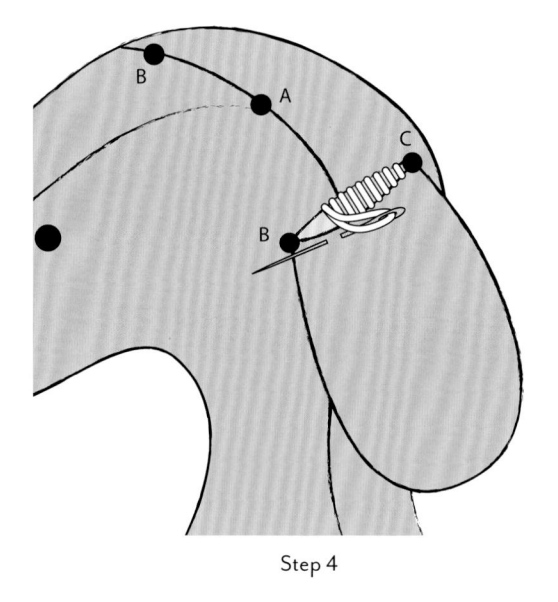

Step 4

HORSE SOFTIE
NEDDYKINS

Finished Size: 9˝ (23cm)

Neddykins is a dependable horse softie that walks on two feet. Neddykins's ears stand tall and upright, so they need a little bit of extra care. Some fabrics are too soft and won't stay up. So, I like to use stiff felt for the ears. If you're using stiff felt, you only need to cut 2 ears. Don't forget some pom-poms or soft felt for a flowing mane that cascades down the horse's neck!

Materials

Plush felt or cuddle fleece: ½ yard (0.5m), or at least 14˝ × 24˝ (35.6 × 61cm)

Pom-poms, 1¼˝ (30mm), black: 4 for mane, option 1

Plush felt: 4˝ × 5˝ (10.2 × 12.7cm) for mane, option 2

Faux leather or felt: 2˝ × 8˝ (5.1 × 20.3cm) for bridle

Stiff felt: 3˝ × 6˝ (7.6 × 15.2cm) for ears (optional)

Yarn: 1 to 2 yards (1 to 2m) for tail

Ribbon, ¼˝ (6mm): 18˝ (45.7cm) for reins (optional)

Sew-in eyes, ¼˝ (6mm): 2

All-purpose thread

Black embroidery thread

Black extra-strong thread

Polyester fiberfill

Standard hand-sewing needle

Large-eyed sewing needle

Long (about 3˝) sewing needle

Long sewing pins

Scissors

Water-erasable fabric pen

Pink or red watercolor pencil (optional)

After you've followed the steps in Preparing to Sew (page 27), it's time to start!

Cutting

Plush felt or cuddle fleece

Cut 1 back with Back.

Cut 2 fronts with Horse Front.

Cut 4 ears with Horse Ear (or none if using optional stiff felt).

Stiff felt (optional)

Cut 2 ears with Horse Ear.

Sewing Neddykins Together

All seam allowances are ¼″ (6mm) unless otherwise noted.

STITCHES NEEDED FOR THIS PROJECT

Backstitch (page 16)

Slip stitch (page 17)

Satin stitch (page 19), optional

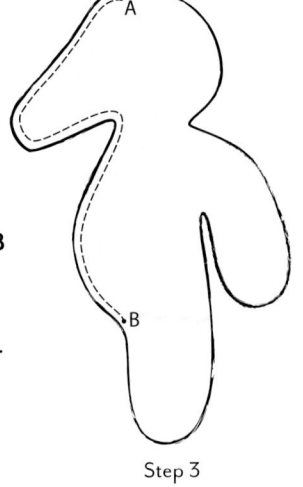

Step 3

1 Place 1 front fabric piece on top of the other with right sides together.

2 Pin the pieces together from dot **A** to dot **B** as marked from the pattern.

3 Thread the needle with all-purpose thread. Neatly sew with a ¼″ (6mm) backstitch from dot **A** to dot **B**. You now have 1 front piece.

4 Lay the front piece flat with the right side facing up.

5 Place the back piece on top of the front piece with right sides together and Neddykins's arms and legs matching. Match the corresponding dots on both pieces, so that dot **A** on the back piece matches dot **A** on the front piece, and so forth for dots **B**, **C**, **D**, **E**, and **F**.

6 Securely pin the front and back pieces together.

7 Sew a ¼″ (6mm) backstitch all the way around both pieces with a ¼″ (6mm) seam allowance, removing the pins as you go. Leave a gap between dot **D** and dot **E** in accordance with the pattern marks. Don't forget to add a double stitch to the start and end of the seam.

8 Check the stitching to ensure that there are no gaps.

9 Turn the softie right side out.

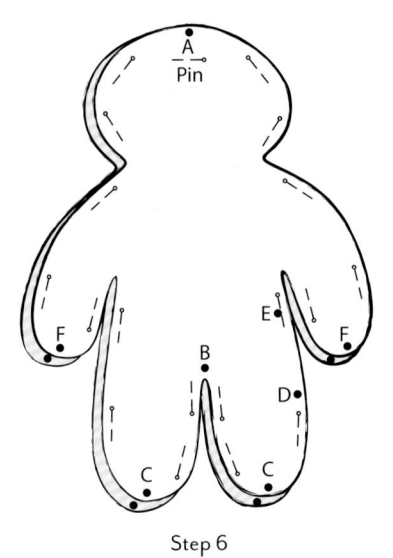

Step 6

Stuffing the Softie

Stuff Neddykins and close the gap as outlined in Stuffing and Finishing the Softies (page 24). Slipstitch from dot **D** to dot **E**.

Adding the Face

Neddykins's face is simple and sweet! You can follow my guidelines to place the eyes, ears, and nose, or choose your own positioning to give your horse a unique personality.

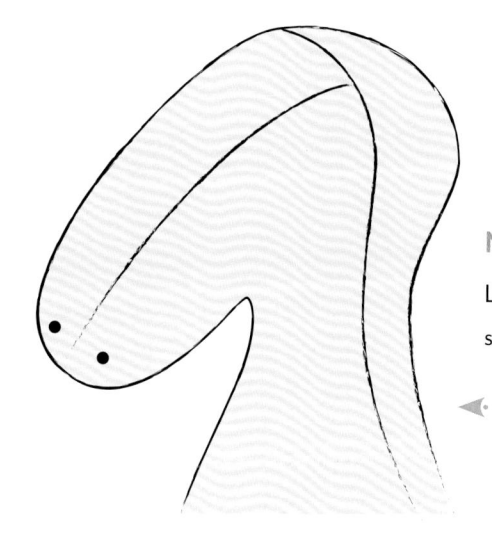

Neddykins's Nose

Look at Neddykins directly. On either side of the long muzzle nose, sew a few small stitches to represent a nostril on each side.

Seams

In order to correctly position the eyes and ears, we're going to refer to the seams on Neddykins. Note the following seams on your softie:

- ♥ Center seam: seam down the middle of the head where the 2 front pieces are sewn together

- ♥ Back seam: seam across the top of the head where the back and front of the head are sewn together

- ♥ Point **A**: spot where the center seam and back seam meet in the middle of the head

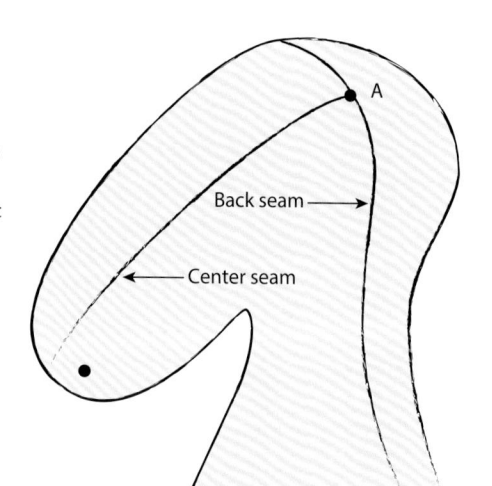

Placing and Sewing Neddykins's Eyes

① Identify point **A** on the top of the softie's head. Measure 1½˝ (3.8cm) from point **A** along the center seam and add a pin to mark point **B**.

② Measure 1˝ (2.5cm) to the left and right of point **B** to identify the placement of each eye (point **C**). Mark each eye with a dot or pin, and then remove the pin for point **B**. Look at your softie to make sure the eye positions are level and evenly spaced from the center seam.

③ Follow the instructions in Sewing the Eyes (page 25) to sew or embroider the eyes onto Neddykins.

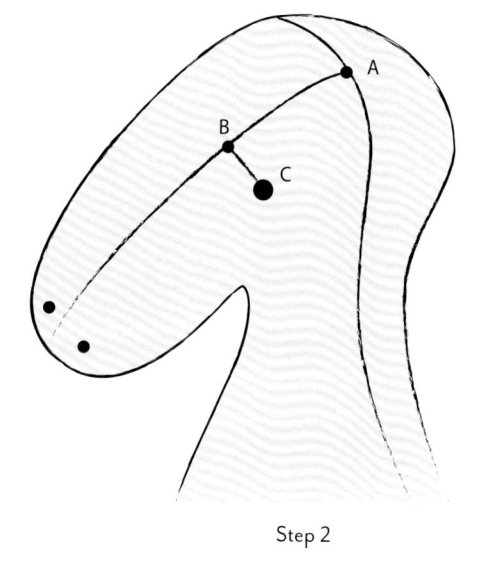

Step 2

Placing and Sewing Neddykins's Ears

If you're using stiff felt you will have only 2 ear pieces. Skip Steps 1 and 2.

1 Divide the 4 ear pieces into pairs. Place them right sides together; then backstitch around the pointed part of each ear, leaving the straight edge open. Don't forget to double stitch at the beginning and end!

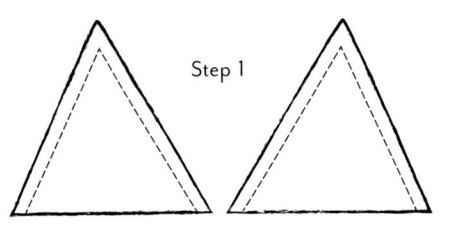

Step 1

2 Turn the ears right side out and fold them in half along the fold line.

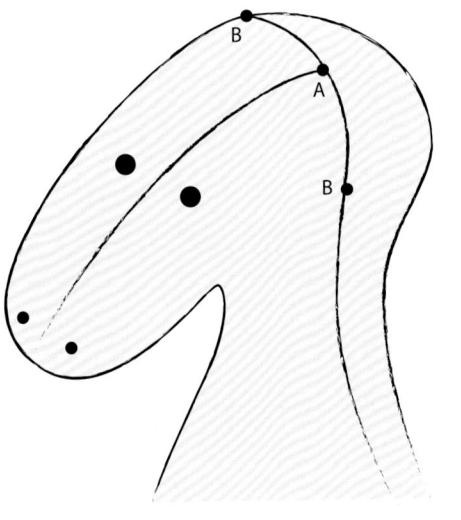

Step 3

3 Identify point **A** on the top of the softie's head. Measure 1.5˝ (3.8cm) from point **A** to the left and right along the back seam and add a pin on each side, creating 2 points **B**.

4 Point **X** is the midpoint of the folded ear at the bottom of the straight edge. Match the **X** to point **B** on the back seam and keep the bottom straight edge horizontal. Pin each ear pointing straight up. Make sure that the ears are level and at the same height.

5 Slipstitch each ear to the head using small stitches.

Step 4

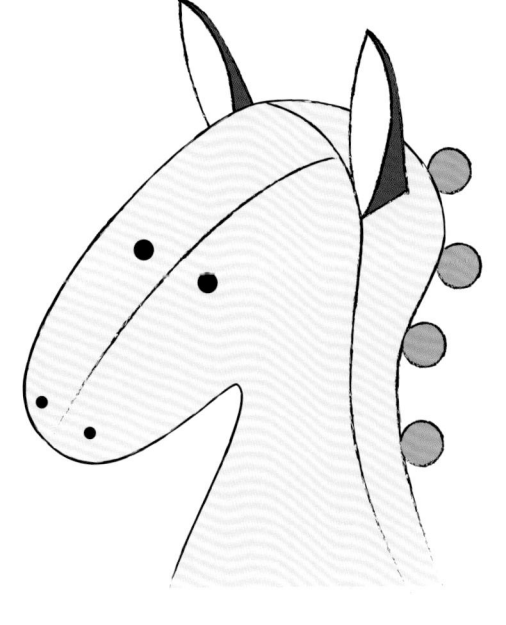

Mane

There are 2 options for the mane for Neddykins.

Mane Option 1

Sew 4 black 1¼˝ (30mm) pom-poms evenly spaced along the back of the neck area to create a stylish mane.

MANE OPTION 2

Fold a 4˝ × 5˝ (10cm × 12.7cm) rectangle of felt in half lengthwise and cut both sides into fringes, with each "strand" of the mane measuring 1½˝ (3.8cm) long and about ¼˝ (6mm) wide. Sew the fringed felt to the back of the neck. The mane should fall on both sides of the softie's neck.

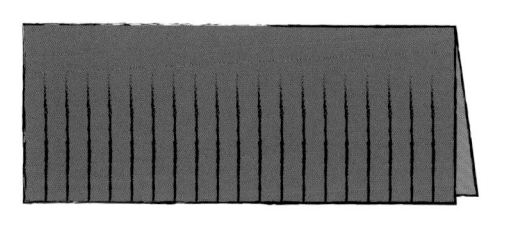

Tail

Cut the yarn into 3 to 6 lengths each measuring 10˝ (25cm). The tail can be thick or thin; the more strands of yarn, the thicker the tail. Fold the strands in half and tie them together, forming a knot in the middle, and trim the ends even. Sew the tail to the horse at the knot.

Bridle

From the faux leather or felt 2˝ × 8˝ (5.1 × 20.3cm) rectangle, cut the following strips:

♥ 1 strip ½˝ × 3½˝ (1.2cm × 8.9cm) for the noseband

♥ 1 strip ½˝ × 7˝ (1.2cm × 17.8cm) for the cheekpieces

♥ 1 strip ½˝ × 4˝ (1.2cm × 10.2cm) for the browband

Test the fit of each piece and trim if necessary. Place the noseband around the horse's nose just above the nostrils. Pin and sew in place under the chin. Attach the cheekpiece strip behind the horse's ears, connecting to each side of the noseband. Pin and sew in place. Place the browband across the forehead of the horse, just in front of the ears and above the eyes, connecting to each cheekpiece. Pin and sew in place.

Try attaching a long piece of bright ribbon to the noseband for the reins. You could also add a few flowers or a feather at the horse's ear for extra decoration, and to cover the bridle stitches (see Flowers!, page 79).

Add color to Neddykins's cheeks if you'd like, using a pink or red watercolor pencil (see Adding Color, page 27); check all the seams and facial features to make sure they're secure; and evenly distribute the fiberfill if any lumps have developed. Neddykins is ready!

Isn't Neddykins fabulous?

Horse Softie: Neddykins

RABBIT SOFTIE

ROBIN

Finished Size: 9˝ (23cm)

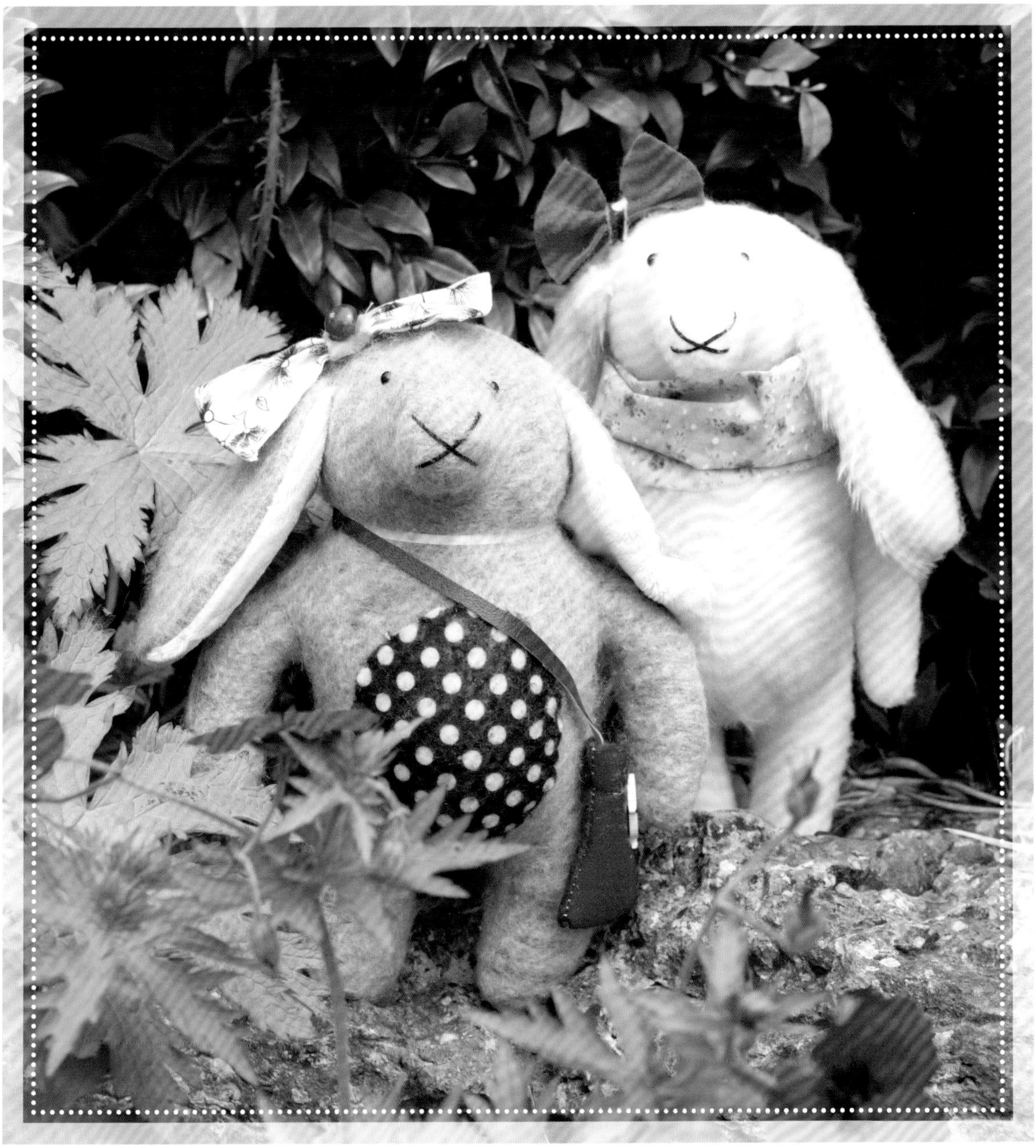

Robin has the cutest floppy ears! Nothing is cuter than a springtime rabbit.

Robin is also especially cute with 2 colored ears and a tummy panel.

After you've followed the steps in Preparing to Sew (page 27), it's time to start!

Materials

Plush felt or cuddle fleece: ½ yard (0.5m), or at least 14˝ × 24˝ (35.6 × 61cm)

White short-pile faux fur: 6˝ × 7˝ (15.2 × 17.8cm) for inner ears (optional)

Contrasting fabric: 4˝ × 5˝ (10.2 × 12.7cm) for tummy panel (optional)

Sew-in eyes, ¼˝ (6mm): 2

All-purpose thread

Black embroidery thread

Pink embroidery thread for nose (optional)

Black extra-strong thread

Polyester fiberfill

Standard hand-sewing needle

Large-eyed sewing needle

Long (about 3˝) sewing needle

Long sewing pins

Scissors

Water-erasable fabric pen

Pink or red watercolor pencil (optional)

Cutting

Plush felt or cuddle fleece

Cut 1 back with Back.

Cut 2 fronts with Rabbit Front.

Cut 4 ears (2 if using optional faux fur) with Rabbit Ear.

Contrasting fabric or white faux fur (optional)

Cut 1 tummy panel with Tummy Panel.

Cut 2 ears with Rabbit ear.

Sewing Robin Together

All seam allowances are ¼˝ (6mm) unless otherwise noted.

STITCHES NEEDED FOR THIS PROJECT

Backstitch (page 16)

Slip stitch (page 17)

Satin stitch (page 19), optional

Whipstitch (page 18), optional

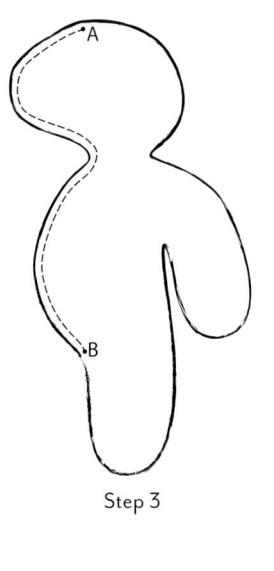

Step 3

1 Place 1 front fabric piece on top of the other with right sides together.

2 Pin the pieces together from dot **A** to dot **B** as marked from the pattern.

3 Thread the needle with all-purpose thread. Neatly sew with a ¼˝ (6mm) backstitch from dot **A** to dot **B**. You now have 1 front piece.

4 Lay the front piece flat with the right side facing up.

5 Place the back piece on top of the front piece with right sides together and Robin's arms and legs matching. Match the corresponding dots on both pieces, so that dot **A** on the back piece matches dot **A** on the front piece, and so forth for dots **B**, **C**, **D**, **E**, and **F**.

6 Securely pin the front and back pieces together.

7 Sew a ¼˝ (6mm) backstitch all the way around both pieces, with a ¼˝ (6mm) seam allowance, removing the pins as you go. Leave a gap between dot **D** and dot **E** in accordance with the pattern marks. Don't forget to add a double stitch to the start and end of the seam.

8 Check the stitching to ensure that there are no gaps.

9 Turn the softie right side out.

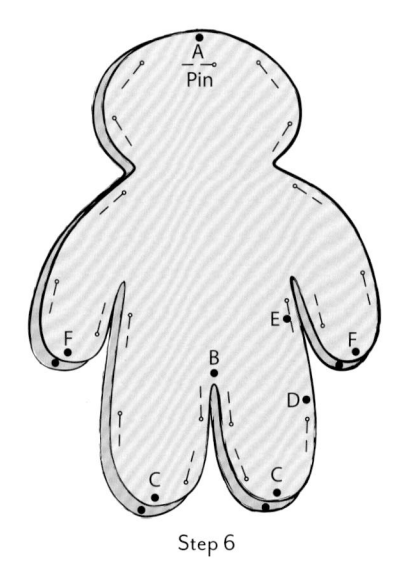

Step 6

Stuffing the Softie

Stuff Robin and close the gap as outlined in Stuffing and Finishing the Softies (page 24). Slipstitch from dot **D** to dot **E**.

Adding the Face

When it comes to maximizing cuteness, creating Robin's face is the most important part of the process! You can follow my guidelines to place the eyes, ears, and nose, or choose your own positioning to give your rabbit a unique personality.

Robin's Nose

To judge the nose position, turn Robin sideways and look at its profile. Plan to position the nose directly at the tip of the muzzle.

Thread the large-eyed needle with black embroidery thread. Sew a large **X** at the tip of the rabbit's muzzle. For a pink triangle nose, paint the fabric in the top part of the **X** with a pink watercolor pencil, or embroider the triangle nose using pink embroidery thread and a satin stitch.

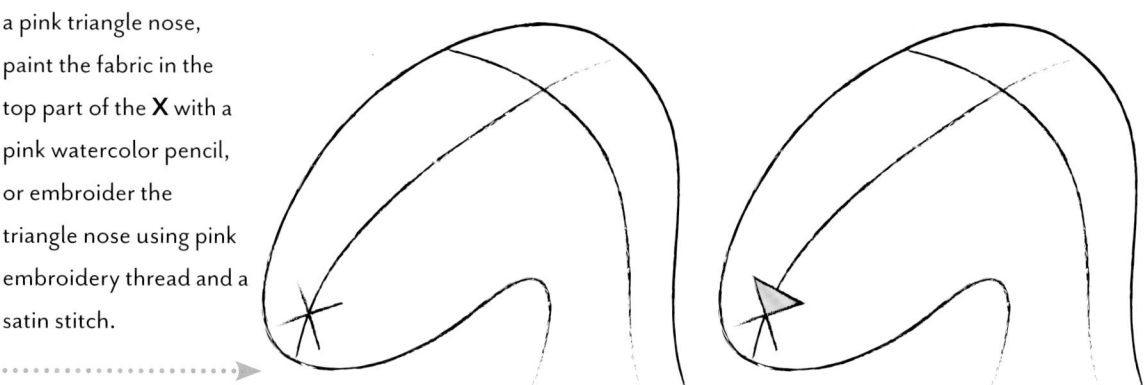

Seams

In order to correctly position the eyes and ears, we're going to refer to the seams on Robin. Note the following seams on your softie:

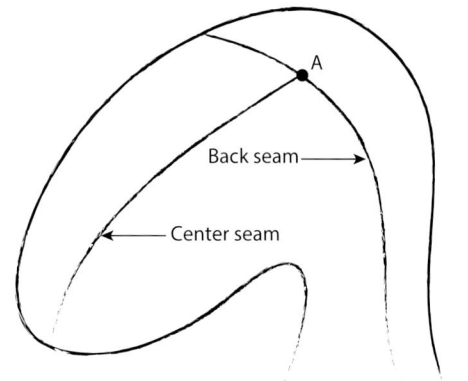

- ♥ Center seam: seam down the middle of the head where the 2 front pieces are sewn together

- ♥ Back seam: seam across the top of the head where the back and front of the head are sewn together

- ♥ Point **A**: spot where the center seam and back seam meet in the middle of the head

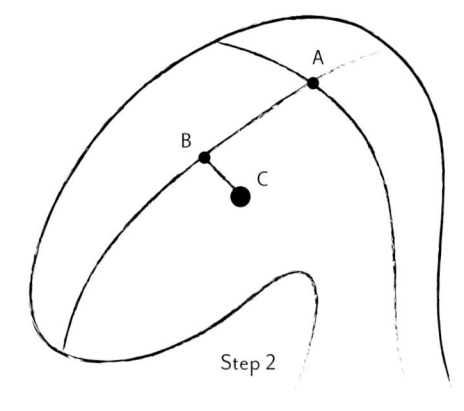

Step 2

Placing and Sewing Robin's Eyes

❶ Identify point **A** on the top of the softie's head. Measure 1˝ (2.5cm) from point **A** along the center seam and add a pin to mark point **B**.

❷ Measure 1˝ (2.5cm) to the left and right of point **B** to identify the placement of each eye (point **C**). Mark each eye with a dot or pin, and then remove the pin for point **B**. Look at the softie to make sure the eyes are level and evenly spaced from the center seam.

❸ Follow the instructions in Sewing the Eyes (page 25) to sew or embroider the eyes onto Robin.

Placing and Sewing Robin's Ears

1. Divide the 4 ear pieces into pairs. Place them right sides together; then backstitch around the curved part of each ear, leaving the bottom edge open. Don't forget to double stitch at the beginning and end!

2. Turn the ears right side out. Fold in the raw edges of the unsewn bottom edge ¼" (6mm); then sew together using small slip stitches.

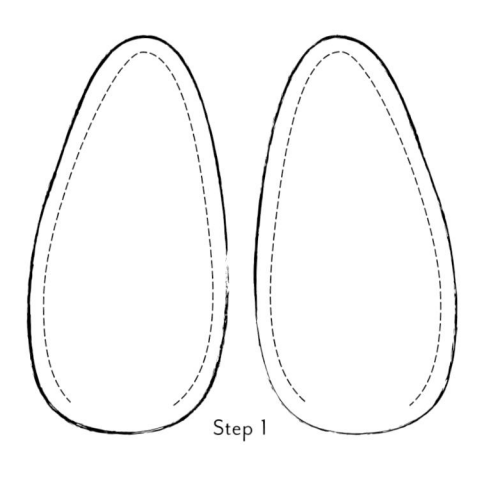

Step 1

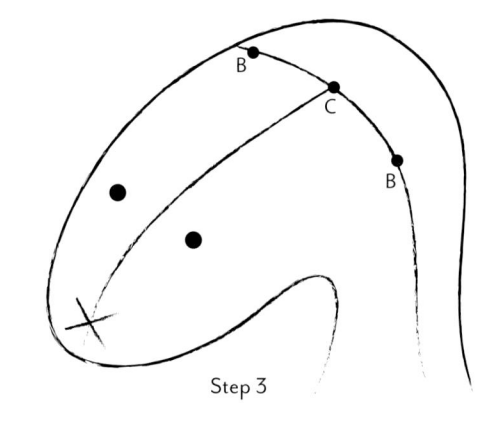

Step 3

3. Identify point **A** on the top of the softie's head. Measure 2" (5.1cm) from point **A** to the left and right along the back seam and add a pin on each side, creating 2 points **B**.

4. Match the **X** on the ear to point **B** on the back seam. Before pinning, make sure the ears are positioned correctly, with the narrow end at the top. Pin in place and make sure the ears are level and at the same height.

5. Slipstitch each ear to the head, using small stitches.

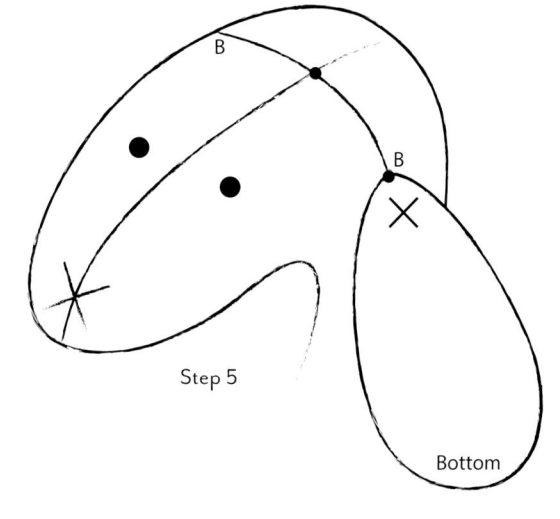

Step 5

Bottom

Tip

If you're using a dark-colored fabric, water down some white or light-colored acrylic paint. Dab the nose and muzzle area with the paint until they have lightened up enough for the nose and mouth to stand out.

If you want, add a tummy panel to Robin, following the instructions in Tummy Panel (page 27). All finished!

Add color to Robin's cheeks if you'd like, using a pink or red watercolor pencil (see Adding Color, page 27); check all the seams and facial features to make sure they're secure; and evenly distribute the fiberfill if any lumps have developed. Robin is ready!

3

Outfits and Accessories

Every softie is cute on its own, but adding accessories is fun and can be a great way to give each animal even more personality. If you're making softies for a young child, consider skipping the accessories or making simple ones, like the ruffle, scarf, and bow, to make sure your final design stays baby-friendly.

These accessories also require very few materials; they're the perfect way to use up scraps!

SHOULDER BAG

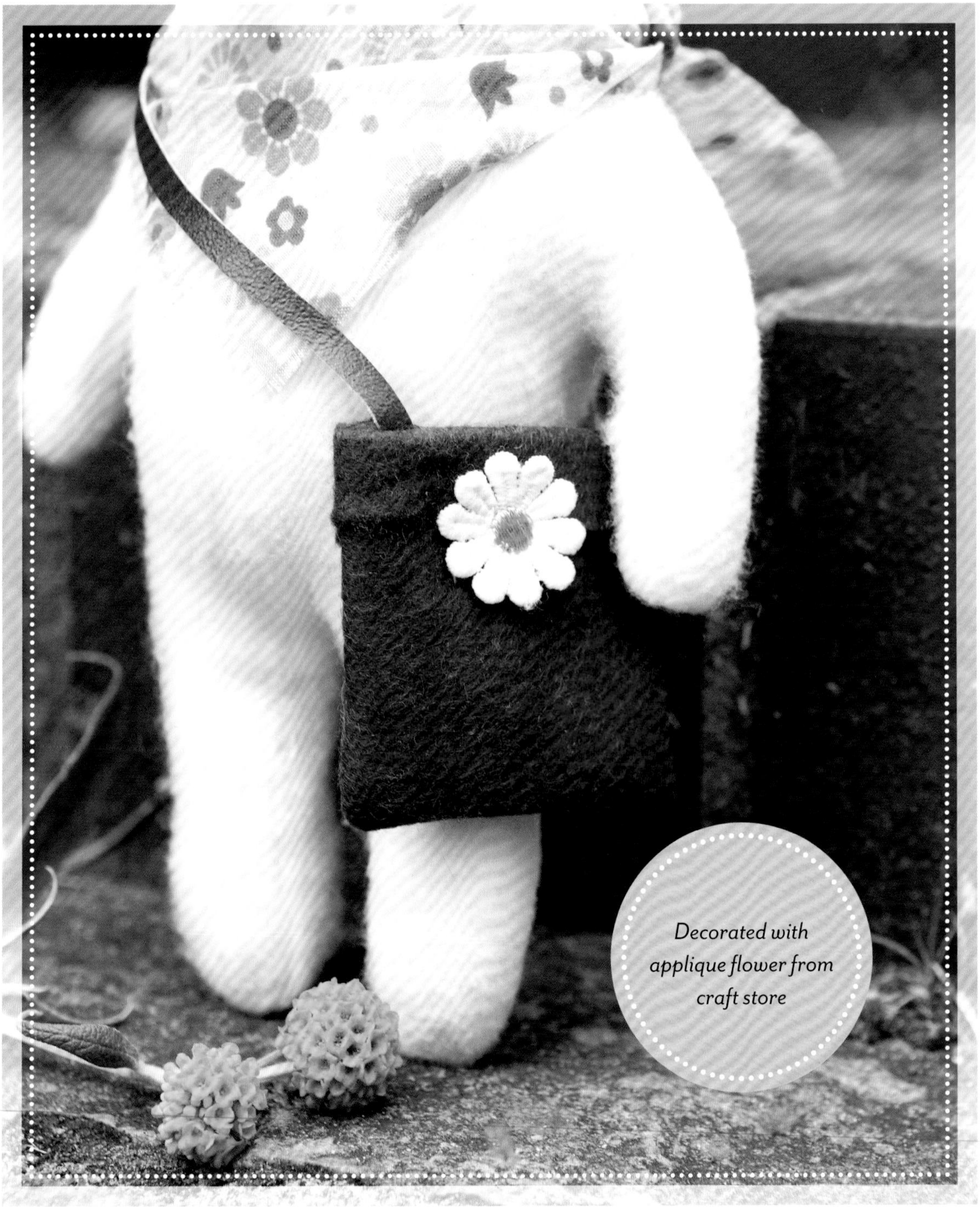

Decorated with applique flower from craft store

Flowers!

Small fabric flowers are great little elements to add to any softie or accessory. Fill a bag with them, stitch them behind an ear, or decorate a scarf with them to make your softie even cuter.

They're simple to make, and all you need are fabric scraps. Cut 6 to 8 flower shapes in different sizes. Each shape can be different and made from a different fabric. Stack the smaller floral shapes on top of the larger shapes, and then sew a few stitches in the center to hold them together. That's it! Stack as many or as few shapes together as you'd like. You can also add a small fabric circle or button in the center of the flower for even more polish.

Materials

Felt: scrap about 4″ × 6″ (10.2 × 15.2cm) for bag

Dark faux leather or felt: 1″ × 12″ (2.5 × 30.5cm) for strap

Scissors

Hand-sewing needle

All-purpose thread

Cutting

Felt

Cut a 3⅛″ × 5½″ (8.3 × 14cm) rectangle.

Dark faux leather or felt

Cut 1 strip ⅝″ × 11″ (1.6 × 27.9cm).

Shoulder Bag Assembly

1 Choose the softie that will be wearing the shoulder bag. Drape the faux leather strap across the softie's shoulder and determine how high or low you want the bag to hang on the body. Trim the strap to match the desired height.

2 Place the 3⅛″ × 5½″ (8.3 × 14cm) felt rectangle so the wrong side is facing up, and turn down a ⅜″ (10mm) hem along the top longer side.

Fold in half, placing the right sides of the fabric together. Pin and sew the raw edges to form a bag measuring 2½″ × 2½″ (6.4 × 6.4cm).

3 Attach the strap to the bag with neat stitches at the places marked with an **X** on the diagram. Make sure the strap is attached securely by double stitching.

4 Turn the bag right side out. All finished! You can fill the bag to match your softie's personality, and even add bows, buttons, or flowers.

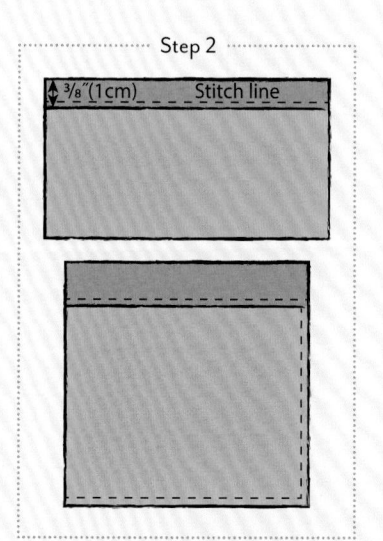

Step 2

⅜″(1cm)   Stitch line

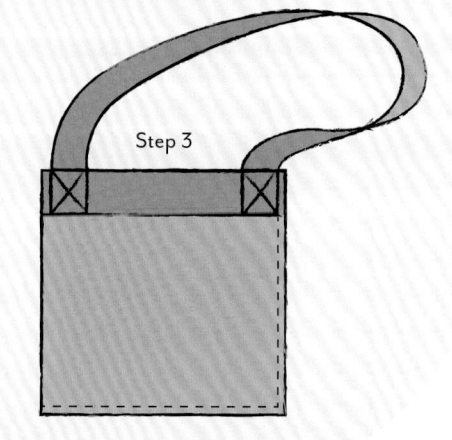

Step 3

Materials

Felt: 3˝ × 11˝ (7.6 × 27.9cm) for a 1-piece collar

Cotton fabric: 6˝ × 11˝ (15.2 × 27.9cm) for a 2-piece collar

Button, ⅜˝ (10mm): 1

Scissors

Hand-sewing needle

All-purpose thread

Cutting

Collar pattern is in Patterns (page 95).

Felt

Cut 1 collar with Collar.

Cotton fabric

Cut 2 collars with Collar, adding a ¼˝ (6mm) seam allowance to all edges.

Collar Assembly

① If you are using felt, fold the collar along the fold line marked on the pattern.

If you are using cotton fabric, place the 2 collar pieces right sides together. Pin and sew all the way around, leaving a small opening on the straight edge for turning. Turn the collar right side out and close the opening with a small slipstitch. Fold the collar along the fold line marked on the pattern.

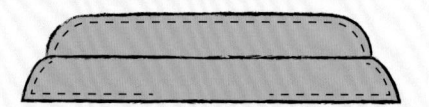

② Test the fit of the collar around the neck of your softie to make sure it fits nicely. Adjust the placement of the button if needed. Thread the needle and sew the button at the spot marked with an **X** on the pattern, or at the location you determined when testing the fit.

③ Cut a small buttonhole slit at the opposite end of the collar, where marked on the pattern.

④ Button the collar around the neck of your softie. For extra accessorizing, tie a bow with ribbon around the collar, or add flowers or lace!

Materials

Light cotton fabric: ⅛ yard (11.4 cm), or at least 3˝ × 30˝ (7.6 × 76.3cm)

Scissors

Hand-sewing needle

All-purpose thread

Cutting

Light cotton fabric

Cut 1 rectangle 3˝ × 30˝ (7.6 × 76.2cm).

Note on Cutting

If you have a pair of pinking or crimping scissors, you can use them to cut out the fabric rectangle. This will give a lovely zigzag edge that provides an alternative to the frayed one shown.

Sewing the Ruffle

1 Lay your fabric rectangle out. If you haven't cut a zigzag edge, lightly fray both long edges of the fabric by teasing out the threads with your fingers. Fold the rectangle in half lengthwise, wrong sides together, matching the frayed edges together.

2 Sew a running stitch all the way along the folded edge, securing the fold. Don't cut the end of the thread off.

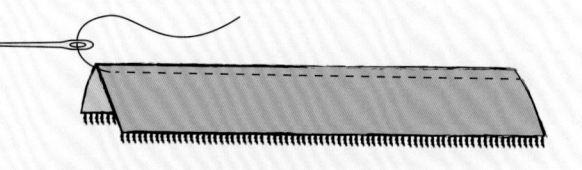

3 Pull on the thread to tighten the running stitch and gather the fabric. It should start to look like a ruffle. Gather the fabric until the ruffle measures 9˝ (22.9cm). Secure by double stitching.

4 Place the ruffle around the neck of the softie so that the ends meet at the back of the neck. Fold under 1 end of the ruffle ¼˝ (6mm) and place it over the other end. Stitch the ends of the ruffle together with slip stitches. Then, sew the ruffle to the back of the neck with a few stitches so that the ruffle stays in place. Add ribbons, flowers, or lace for extra fun!

SCARF

Materials

Plush felt, cuddle fleece, or cotton: ⅛ yard (11.4 cm), or at least 4″ × 15″ (10.2 × 38.1cm)

Scissors

Hand-sewing needle

All-purpose thread

Sewing pins

Snap fastener or hook-and-loop tape dot: 1 small (optional)

Cutting

Plush felt, cuddle fleece, or cotton

Cut 1 rectangle 4″ × 15″ (10.2 × 38.1cm).

Sewing the Scarf

For plush felt or cuddle fleece, skip Step 1.

① Fold over the cotton fabric ⅜″ (10mm) on all sides. Pin and sew a small hem all the way around the rectangle using a whipstitch.

② Starting with a secure double stitch, sew a running stitch from corner **A** to corner **C**. Pull the thread to form gathers until the scarf measures 2″ (5.1cm). Double stitch to secure the tension and the gathers.

③ Repeat Step 3 for the other short edge, from corner **B** to corner **D.**

④ Between points **B** and **D**, sew in a snap fastener or hook-and-loop tape dot on the wrong side of the fabric.

⑤ Turn the scarf over so the right side is facing up, and sew the other half of the snap fastener or hook-and-loop tape dot on the right side of the fabric between points **A** and **C.** Attach the scarf to your softie! Alternatively, you can sew the scarf together with a few stitches instead of using a fastener.

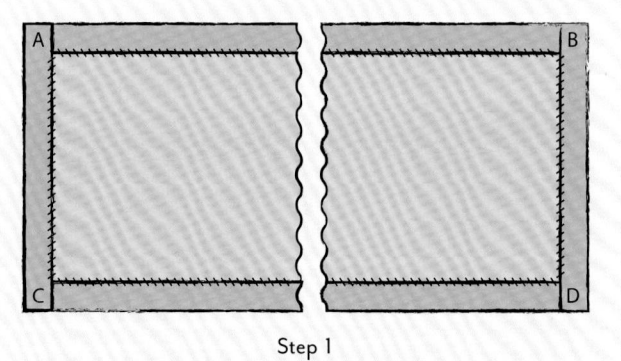

Step 1

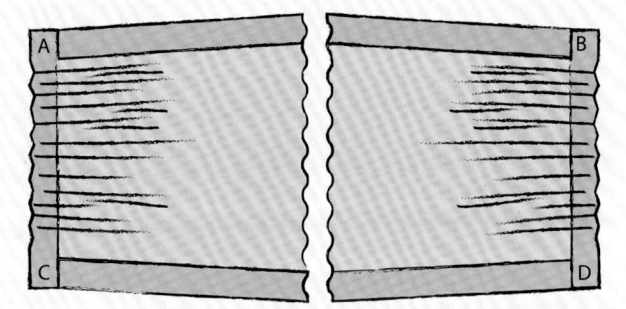

Step 3: Gather each end until it is 2″ wide.

SHAWL

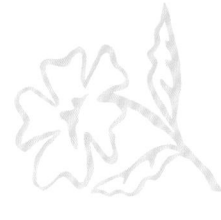

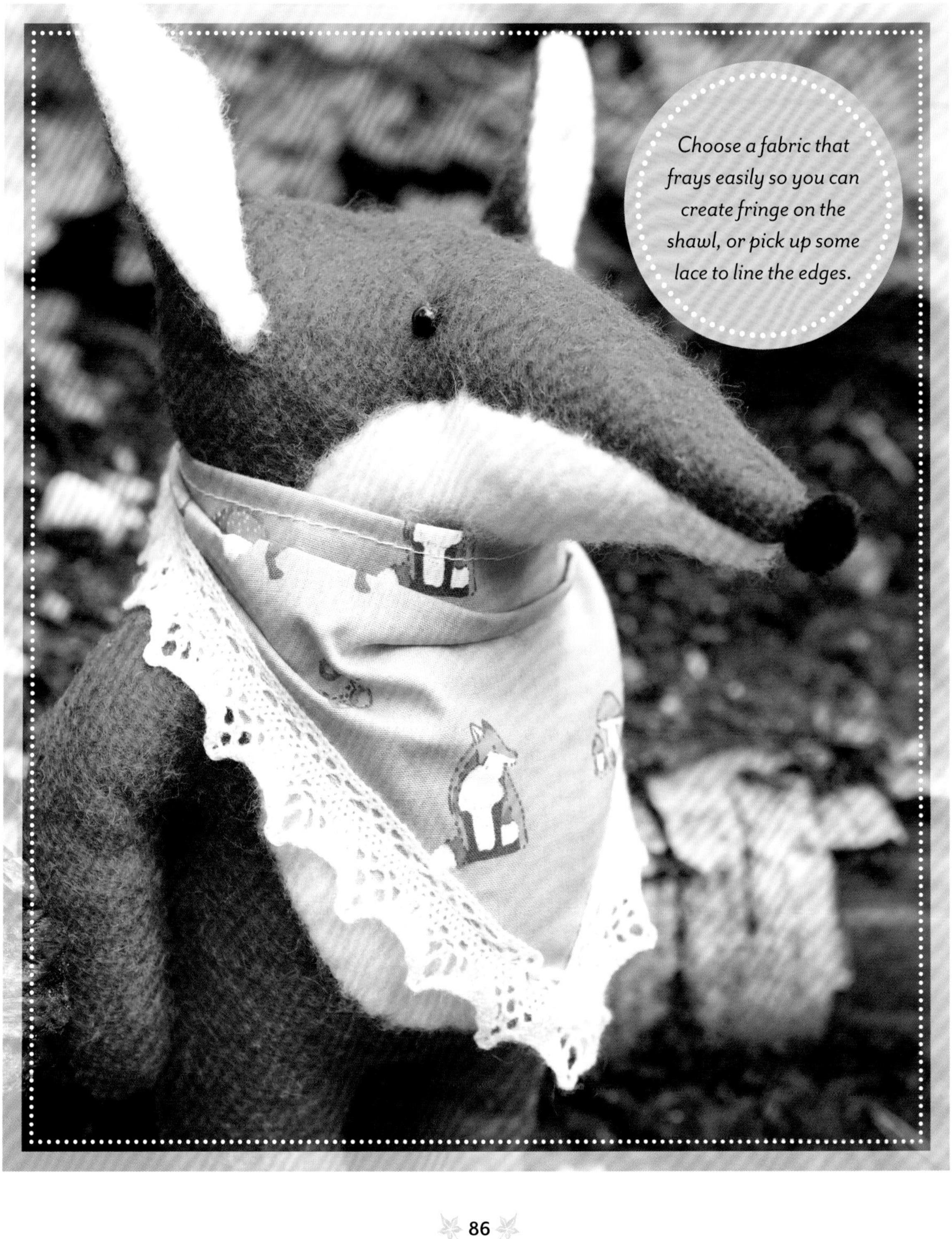

Choose a fabric that frays easily so you can create fringe on the shawl, or pick up some lace to line the edges.

Materials

Cotton or woven fabric: ¼ yard (22.9cm),
or at least 6˝ × 12˝ (15.2 × 30.5cm)

Scissors

Hand-sewing needle

All-purpose thread

Sewing pins

Shawl Assembly

1 Lay the fabric out with the wrong side facing up.
Fold the rectangle in half to create a square that
measures 6˝ × 6˝ (15.2 × 15.2cm).

2 Fold the square in half again to form a right triangle,
with 2 sides still measuring 6˝ (15.2cm).

3 Cut through the fold along the long side of the
triangle, from **A** to **B**. You will now have a triangle with
2 sides measuring 8½˝ (21.6cm) and the long side
measuring 12˝ (30.5cm).

4 Fray the edges of the fabric on the 2 shorter sides of
the triangle by gently teasing out the threads to create a
fringe, or sew ribbon or lace to the shorter sides of the
shawl for a posher look. Place the shawl around your
softie's neck and tie a knot at the back to secure it.

Cutting

Cotton or woven fabric

Cut 1 rectangle 6˝ × 12˝ (15.2 × 30.5cm).

Step 1

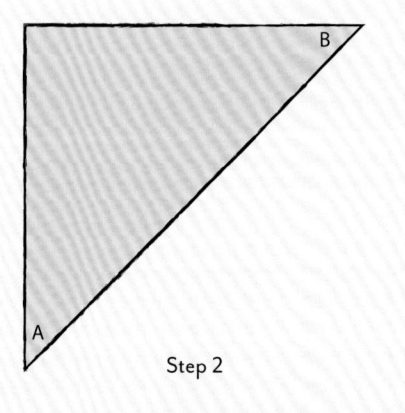

Step 2

Step 3: Cut along fold from A to B.

Materials

Felt: 7″ × 7″ (17.8 × 17.8cm) square

Scrap felt or ribbon: 6″ for hat band

Scissors

Hand-sewing needle

All-purpose thread

Sewing pins

Polyester fiberfill

Water-erasable fabric pen

Cutting

Hat pattern pieces are in Patterns (page 108). There are 2 brim sizes for the hat. Make sure you select either the small or medium brim size and cut only 1 from the felt.

Felt

Cut 1 rectangle 2½″ × 5¼″ (6.4 × 13.3cm) for crown.

Cut 1 top circle with Top of Hat.

Cut 1 hat brim with Small Hat Brim **or** Medium Hat Brim.

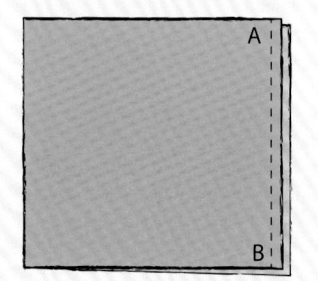

Step 1

Top Hat Assembly

1 Fold fabric in half with right sides together, matching the short edges. Pin and sew from **A** to **B**.

2 Open the crown so that you have a short cylinder. Insert the top-of-hat circle into the top of the cylinder and pin the 2 pieces together. Pinning these 2 pieces together might be trickier than pinning 2 flat pieces together. Insert the first pin at point **1** and continue numerically according to the diagram (right). If any gaps remain, add additional pins before continuing.

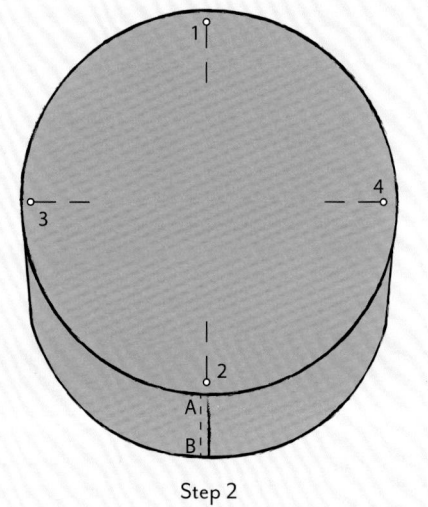

Step 2

3 Stitch the top circle to the cylinder with a running stitch. Turn the hat right side out, and add a small amount of loose stuffing to form an upright hat top.

4 Place the hat top on the center of the fabric brim circle. Pin so that the brim is even on all sides of the hat top. Sew in place using a small running stitch.

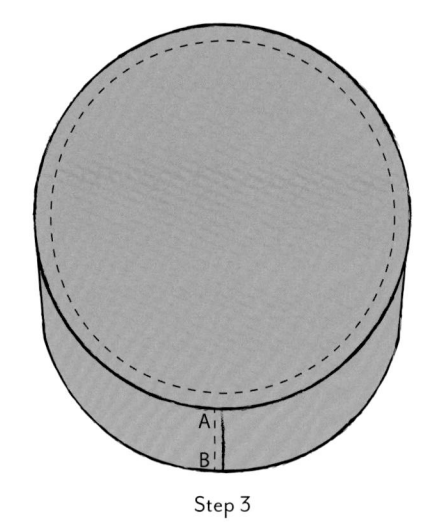

Step 3

Step 4

5 Attach a thin strip of felt or a ribbon as a hat band to cover the running stitch. Add flowers, bows, or additional ribbons for extra fun decoration. My favorite addition is a feather.

Step 5

Top Hat

BOW

Materials

Felt: 4″ × 7″ (10.2 × 17.8cm)

Scissors

Hand-sewing needle

All-purpose thread

Cutting

Felt

Cut 1 rectangle 3″ × 4¾″
(7.6 × 12.1cm) for the bow.

Cut 1 rectangle 1″ × 2″ (2.5 × 5.1cm) for the center.

Note on Size

Bows can be made any size. The measurements here make a large bow. For a smaller bow, cut 1 rectangle 2″ × 3″ (5.1 × 7.6cm), and cut the center strip ⅕″ × 2″ (1.3 × 5.1cm).

Bow Assembly

1 Fold the bow rectangle in half lengthwise so that it measures 4¾″ × 1½″ (12.1 × 3.8cm).

2 Fold both long edges down to the fold line to pleat the bow.

3 Pinch in the middle of the folded rectangle, and then sew a few stitches to firmly secure the folds and the bow shape.

4 Wrap the small felt rectangle around the middle of the bow, covering the stitches, and sew closed at the back. Attach to your softie with a few stitches wherever it best suits the animal's personality!

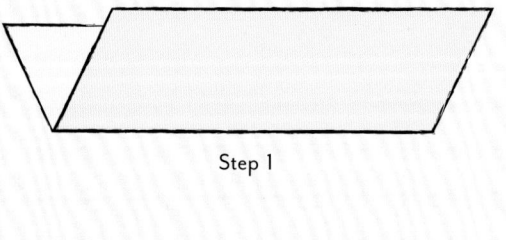

Step 1

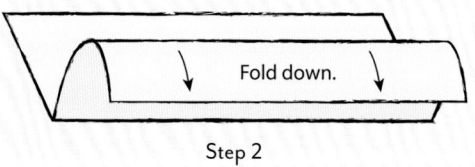

Fold down.

Step 2

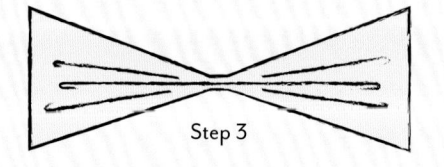

Step 3

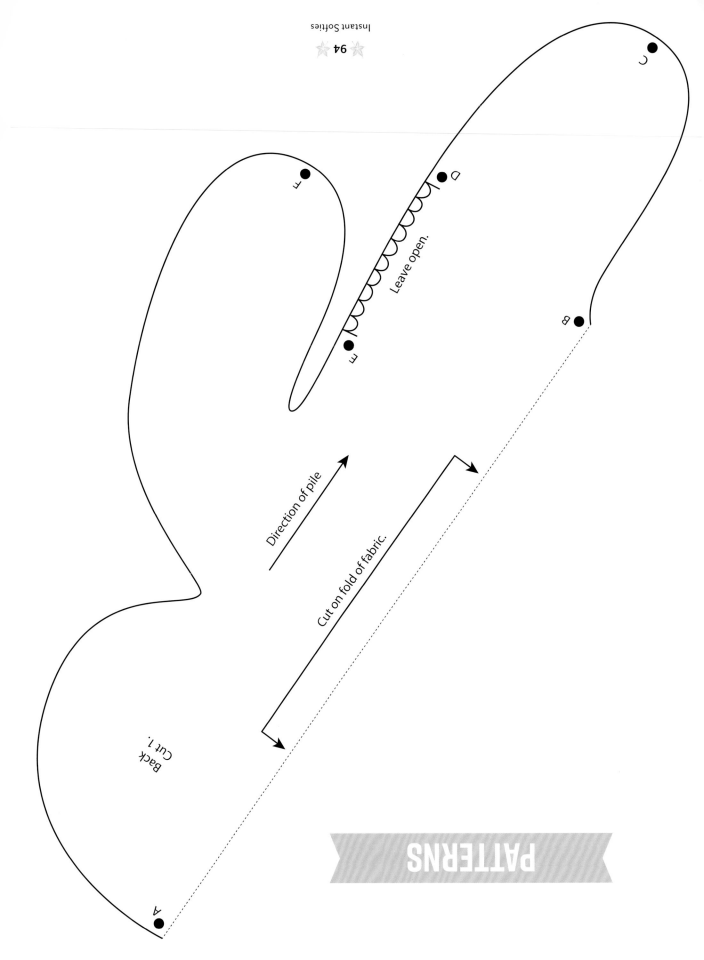

Direction of pile

Cut on fold of fabric.

Leave open.

Back
Cut 1.

A

B

C

D

E

F

PATTERNS

Cut 1 felt.
Cut 2 in cotton.

Collar

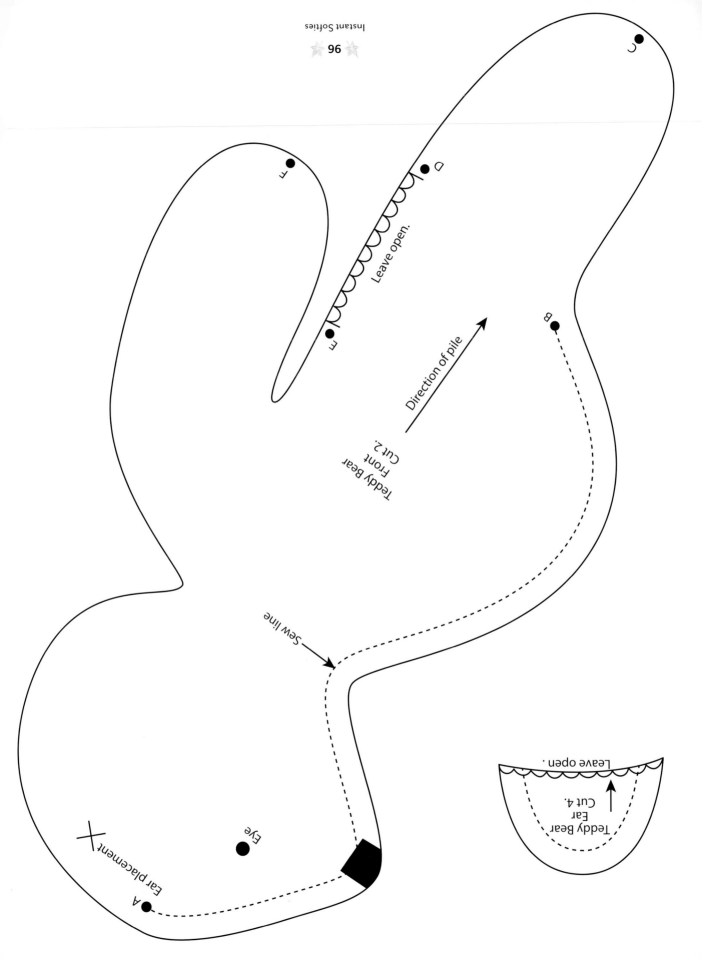

Leave open.

Direction of pile

Teddy Bear
Front
Cut 2.

Sew line

Ear placement

A

Eye

Teddy Bear
Ear
Cut 4.

Leave open.

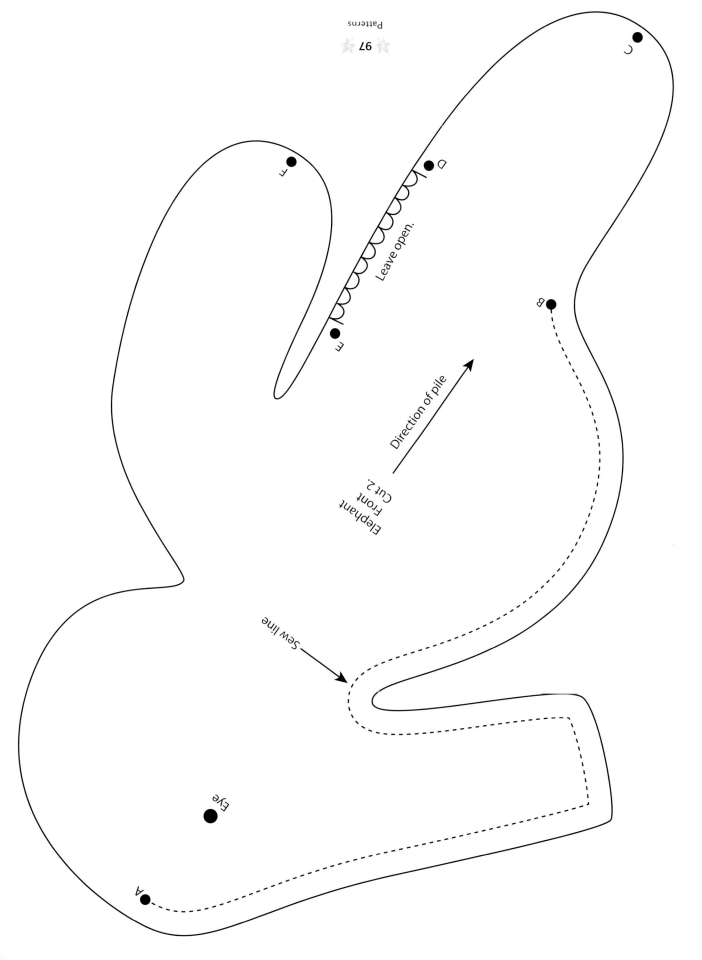

Leave open.

Direction of pile

Elephant
Front
Cut 2.

Sew line

Eye

A

B

C

D

E

F

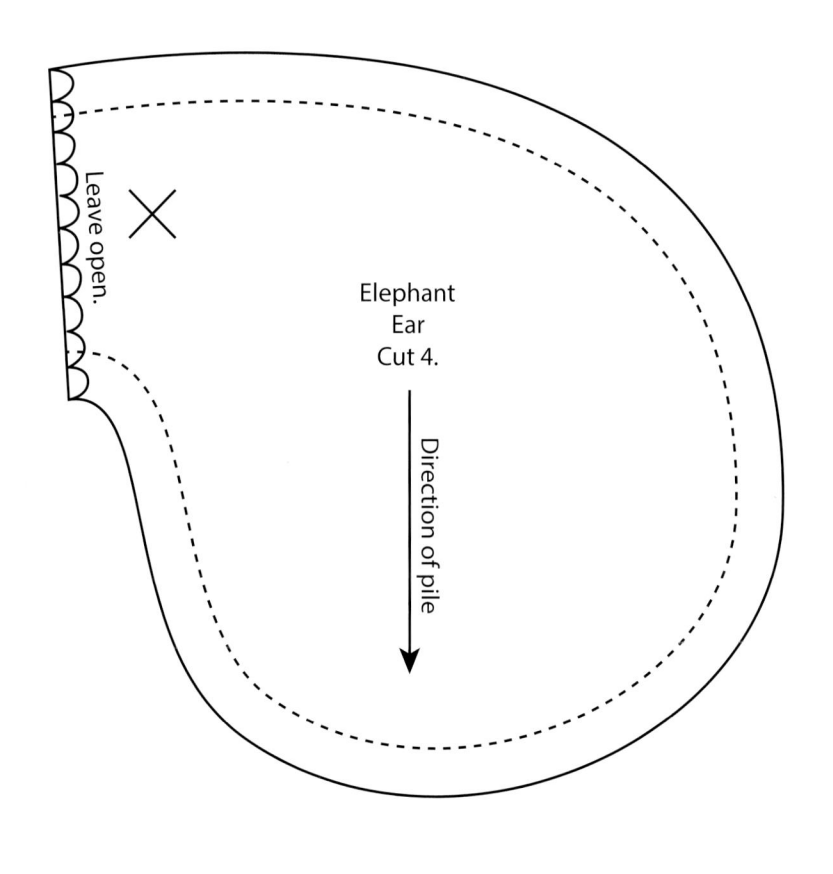

Leave open.

Elephant
Ear
Cut 4.

Direction of pile

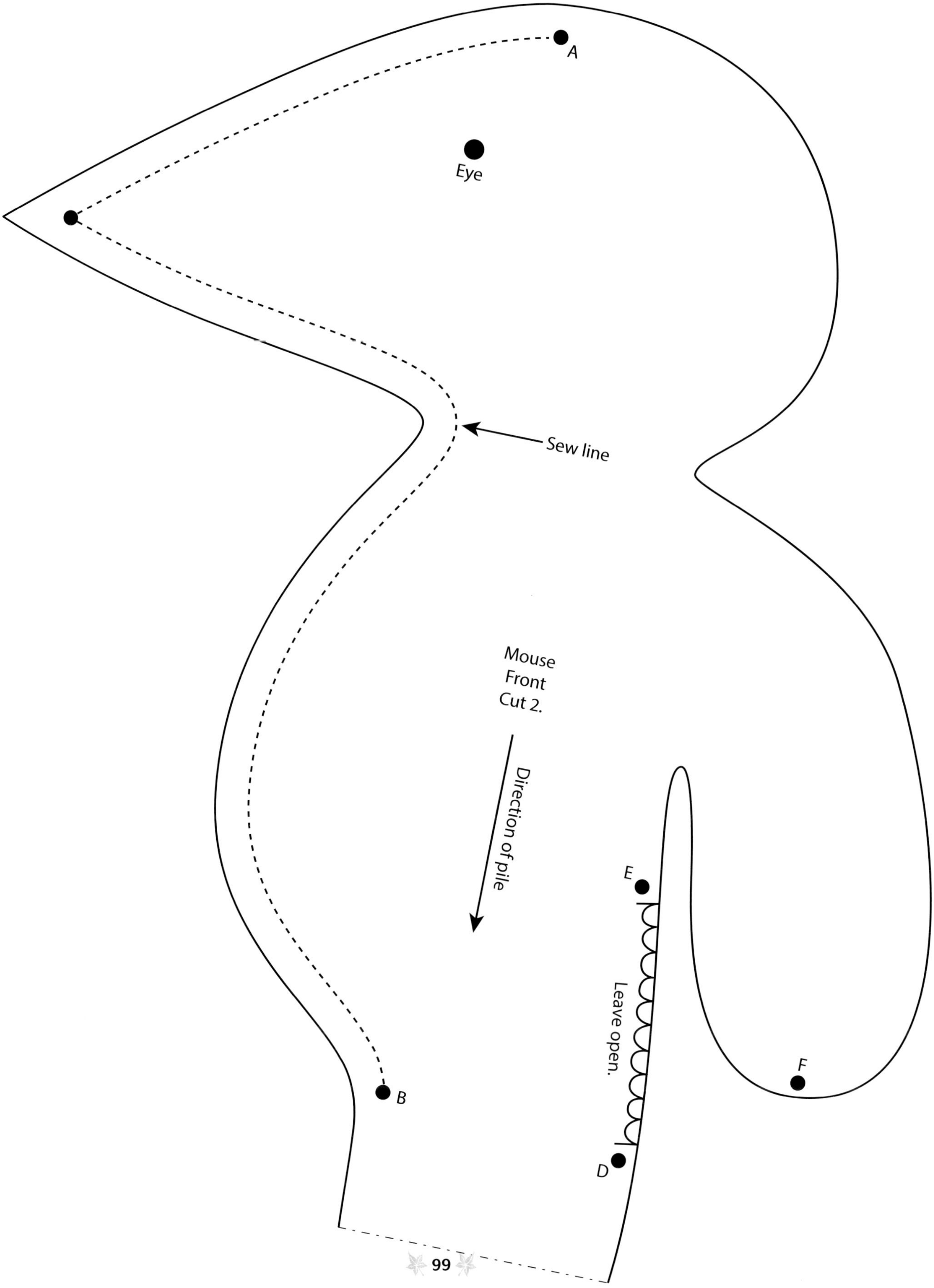

A

Eye

Sew line

Mouse
Front
Cut 2.

Direction of pile

E

Leave open.

B

D

F

Patterns

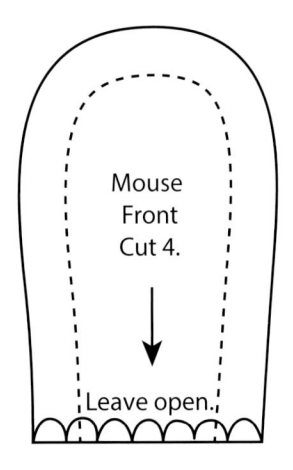

Mouse
Front
Cut 4.

Leave open.

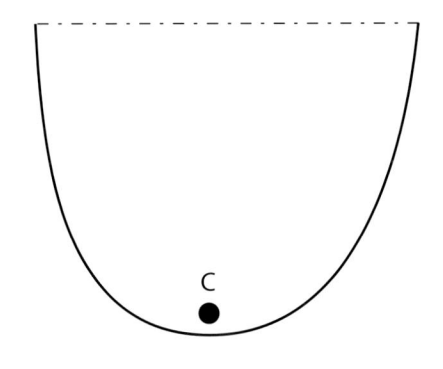

C

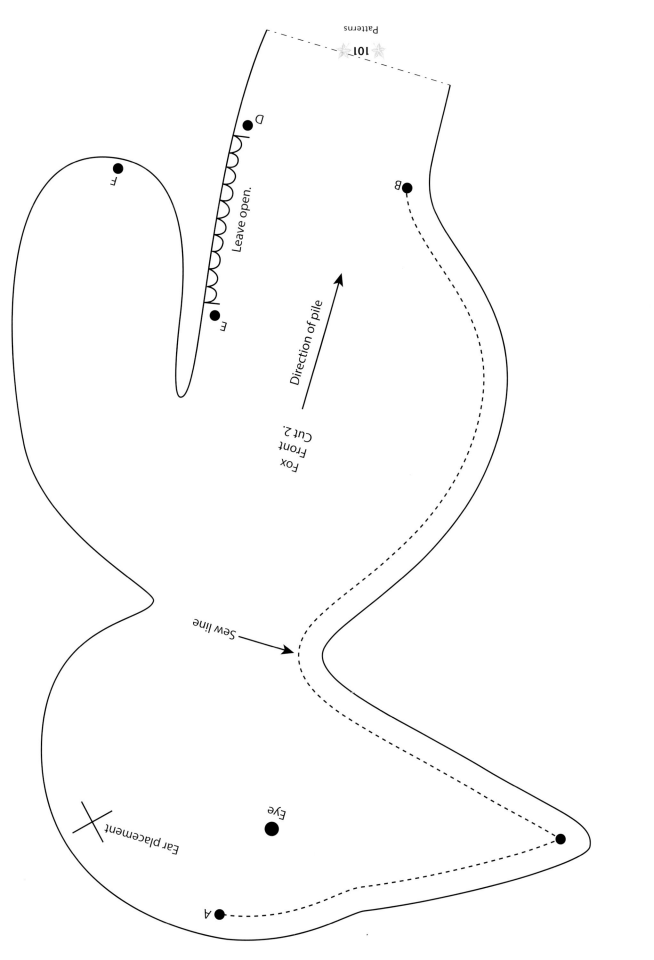

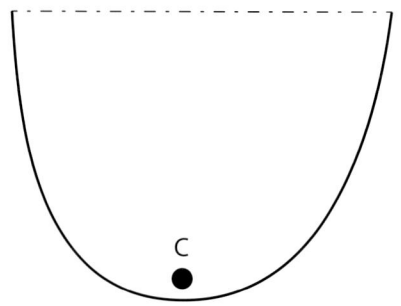

Fox
Ear
Cut 4.

Leave open.

C

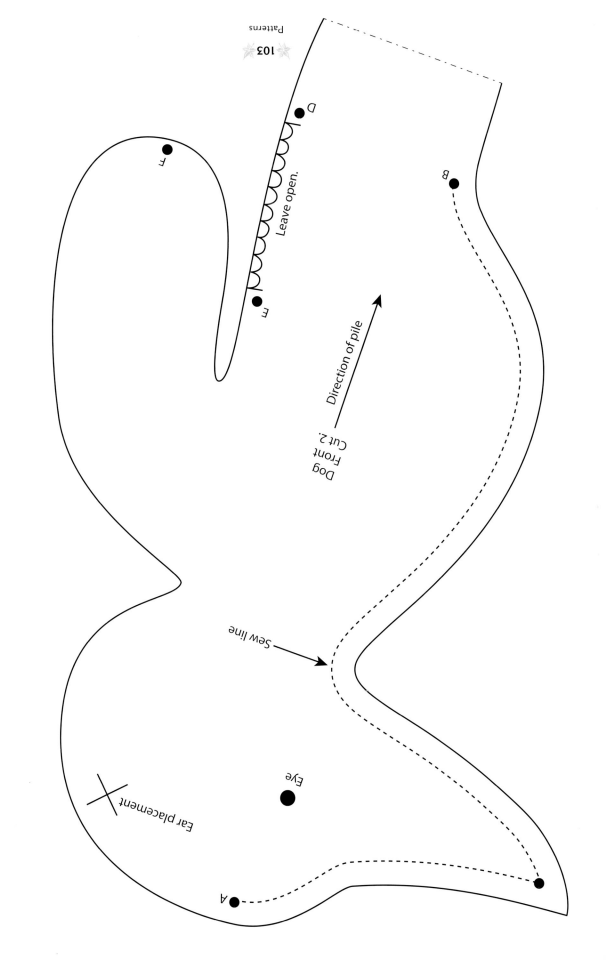

D

Leave open.

E

F

Direction of pile

Dog
Front
Cut 2.

Sew line

Ear placement

Eye

A

B

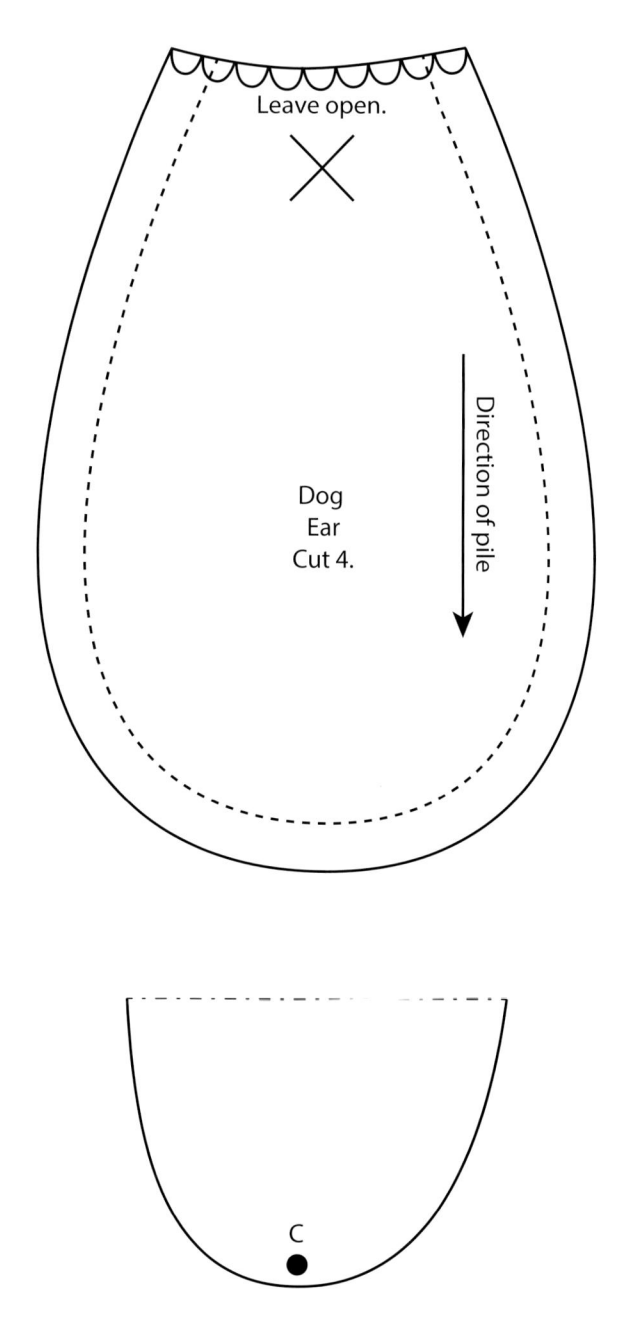

Leave open.

Direction of pile

Dog
Ear
Cut 4.

C

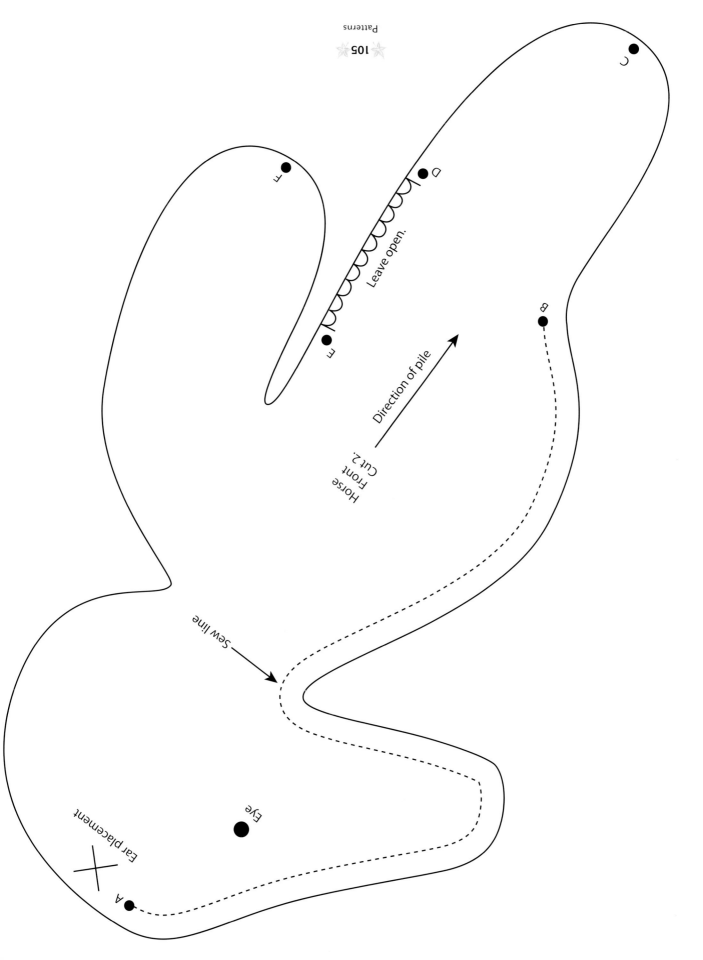

Horse
Front
Cut 2.

Direction of pile

Leave open.

Sew line

Ear placement

Eye

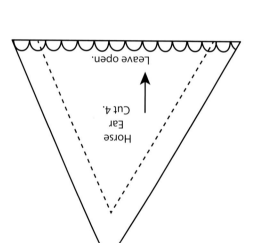

Horse
Ear
Cut 4.

Leave open.

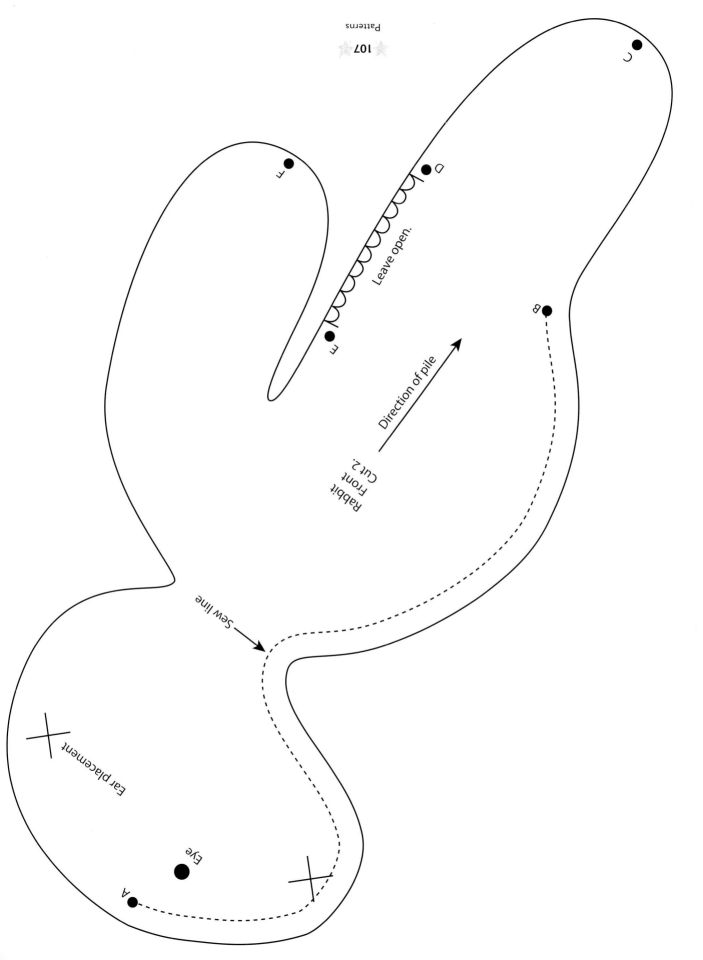

Rabbit
Front
Cut 2.

Direction of pile

Leave open.

Sew line

Ear placement

Eye

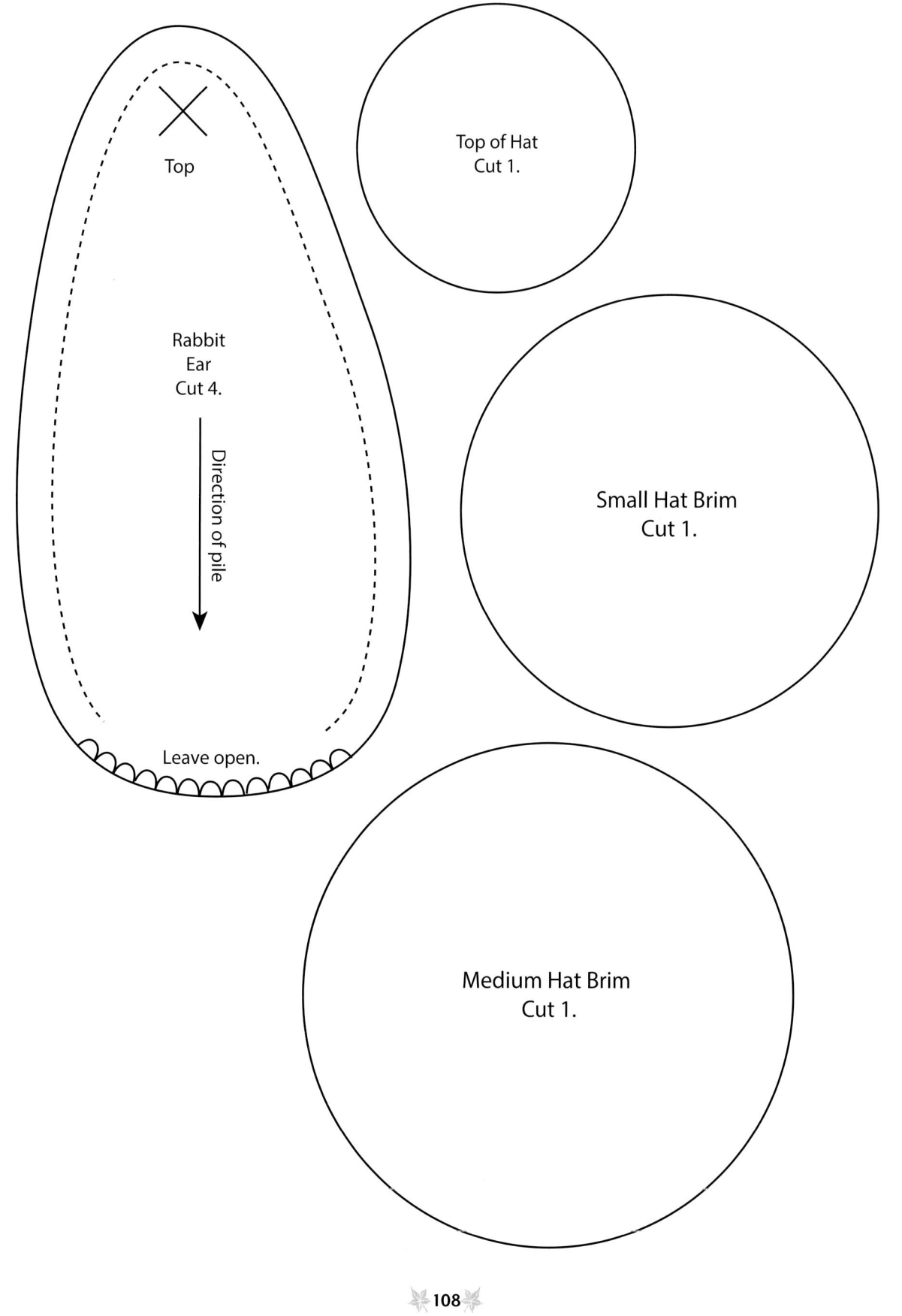

Top

×

Rabbit
Ear
Cut 4.

Direction of pile

Leave open.

Top of Hat
Cut 1.

Small Hat Brim
Cut 1.

Medium Hat Brim
Cut 1.

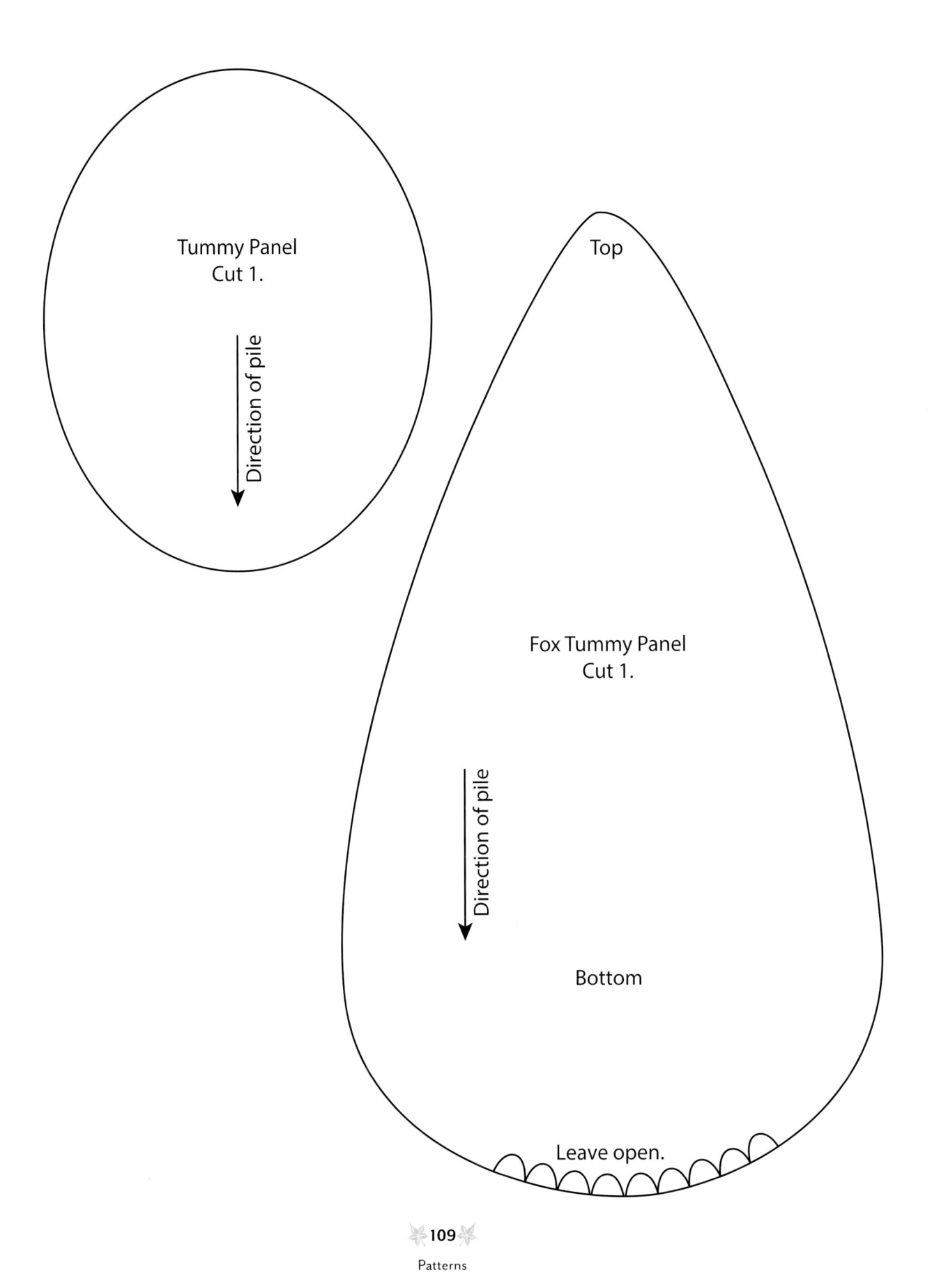

Tummy Panel
Cut 1.

Direction of pile

Top

Fox Tummy Panel
Cut 1.

Direction of pile

Bottom

Leave open.

ABOUT THE AUTHOR

Isabelle Ewing lives in Northern Ireland, just outside of Belfast. She has a lifelong love of drawing, painting and sewing. She is a seasoned crafter, and spends time designing and making cloth dolls, bears, and papier màchê figures. Isabelle wants everyone to experience how satisfying it is to be creative, and is committed to sharing her love of crafting with easy-to-follow instructions and clear illustrations.

Photo by Isabelle Ewing

She has sold artwork to local shops, and at the beautiful Victorian St. Georges market in the heart of the city. Her sculptural work has been exhibited in the Bristol Museum. Charming Softies is her first book.

CREATIVE
SPARK
ONLINE LEARNING

Crafty courses to become an expert maker...

From their studio to yours, Creative Spark instructors are teaching you how to create and become a master of your craft. So not only do you get a look inside their creative space, you also get to be a part of engaging courses that would typically be a one or multi-day workshop from the comfort of your home.

Creative Spark is not your one-size-fits-all online learning experience. We welcome you to be who you are, share, create, and belong.

Scan for a gift from us!

creativespark.ctpub.com